simple secrets to
a happy life

Luci Swindoll

NELSON
BOOKS

An Imprint of Thomas Nelson

Published in Nashville, Tennessee, by Nelson Books, an imprint of Thomas Nelson. Nelson Books and Thomas Nelson are registered trademarks of HarperCollins Christian Publishing, Inc.

Thomas Nelson titles may be purchased in bulk for educational, business, fund-raising, or sales promotional use. For information, please e-mail SpecialMarkets@ThomasNelson.com.

Page design by Mandi Cofer.

Unless otherwise indicated, Scripture quotations are taken from *The Message*. Copyright © by Eugene H. Peterson 1993, 1994, 1995, 1996, 2000, 2001, 2002. Used by permission of Tyndale House Publishers, Inc.

Scripture quotations marked KJV are from the King James Version. Public domain.

Scripture quotations marked NASB are from New American Standard Bible®. Copyright © 1960, 1962, 1963, 1968, 1971, 1972, 1973, 1975, 1977, 1995 by The Lockman Foundation. Used by permission. (www.Lockman.org)

Scripture quotations marked NIV are from the Holy Bible, New International Version®, NIV®. Copyright © 1973, 1978, 1984, 2011 by Biblica, Inc.™ Used by permission of Zondervan. All rights reserved worldwide. www.zondervan.com. The "NIV" and "New International Version" are trademarks registered in the United States Patent and Trademark Office by Biblica, Inc.™

Scripture quotations marked NLT are from the *Holy Bible*, New Living Translation. © 1996, 2004, 2007, 2013 by Tyndale House Foundation. Used by permission of Tyndale House Publishers, Inc., Carol Stream, Illinois 60188. All rights reserved.

Scripture quotations marked NKJV are from the New King James Version®. © 1982 by Thomas Nelson. Used by permission. All rights reserved.

The source of some of the maxims and statements quoted in this volume are not known. Readers who can document the source are asked to contact the publisher so correct attribution can be added to future printings.

ISBN 978-0-310-62458-5 (custom)

Library of Congress Cataloging-in-Publication Data

Swindoll, Luci, 1932-
Simple secrets to a happy life / Luci Swindoll.
   p. cm.
ISBN 978-1-4002-0353-6
1. Christian life. 2. Conduct of life. 3. Happiness--Religious aspects--Christianity. I. Title.
BV4501.3.S965 2012
248.4--dc23

                                    2011038357

Printed in the United States of America
15 16 17 18 19 RRD 6 5 4 3 2

*To my mother, Lovell Lundy Swindoll, who died forty
years ago at the age of sixty-three while writing a
book she never finished. In her honor, I dedicate this
book to her. In the front of Mother's Bible, which she
read every day, was this verse: "That our sons may be
as plants grown up in their youth; that our daughters
may be as corner stones, polished after the similitude
of a palace" (Psalm 144:12 KJV). She prayed and
believed that for both of my brothers and me.*

Contents

Contents

Part Four: Living a Good Life

Part Five: Staying Connected

{ FOREWORD }

An Immersion in Matters of the Soul

If you knew Luci Swindoll, you would know that there is no way to capture her in a way that does justice to that crystalline mind of hers, her exuberance and wild spirit, her great huge tender heart. I'm not going to try, even on the occasion of *Simple Secrets to a Happy Life*, her marvelous, rich new book. But there are a few things I can share with you about her.

I have known her intimately for a dozen or so years. I adore her, and yes, that profound faith of hers is one thing I love, something that has, in her books, helped me more over the years than I can say. Yes, her hilarious sense of humor and timing are so delight-ful—sometimes gentle, sometimes acerbic—that they cause me to feel simultaneously blessed and jealous. There's no one kinder. And of course, she can casually recite to you one of the world's most significant poems, render it elegant and accessible at the same time, blow you away with her ability to have memorized so many of the great poems of all time, which you've just *got* to love in a person—especially if you yourself have grown to be someone who can barely remember to take your socks off before getting in the shower. Here she is, reciting "Sailing to Byzantium," or a Shakespearean sonnet, without being a show-off about it—but instead because she is a giver of light, and the poem maybe amplifies a point of faith or history that you were talking about.

Now, normally, I do not like to be around people who are quite so highly accomplished, because it makes me feel somewhat inadequate. I'm a drop-out, while here she was a cartographer for Mobil Oil, and sang opera professionally, and has read every single literary classic, and can discuss them, and make you laugh during this discussion, plus throw the lights on for you, AND on top of it all, speaks to gigantic audiences as a member of the Women of Faith, and has written a dozen books of her own, and blah blah blah. What *ev*, as the teenagers say. But I forgive Luci's accomplishments because while she's a classicist, she's also totally cool, actively cool—and I don't just mean the haircut. She's *au courant* with the great music, poetry, and issues of our time, even while rattling off Edna St. Vincent Millay. The thing is that around Luci, you're not with someone who is giving herself airs, but rather someone who is an agent for the life-giving artistic coolness of God, the way a clarinet is an agent for the Mozart concerto.

So, here's the problem: we met a dozen or so years ago, when I had lunch with the Women of Faith, and of course I fell in love with them all because, I tell you, they make a girl weak in the knees, and I wanted to follow them around for the rest of my life like a little dog, lapping up their joyful, contagious Christian wisdom. And then there was Luci. She's sturdy, maybe zaftig, stylishly white haired, beautiful as a model, a font of knowledge and faith, and yet one of life's great listeners, who made me laugh and who clearly thought I was the funniest, snappiest piece of cheese in the world.

Naturally, I thought it meant we were soul mates.

And I have felt this ever since I met her, that we have a special connection of the heart and soul, as women who love to read and laugh and write and dance and be silly, who both love to hide in their studies and travel the world, who love their friends and their solitude, more than anything on earth, except for our guy Jesus. We've become dear friends. I know I could call her from anywhere in the world and ask her for help—to wire me funds, or simply listen, to pray with me and share the exact right line of Scripture, or make me laugh about our shared humanity and occasional ridiculousness. But the soul mate thing is ever so slightly more complicated because it turns out she has this effect on *everyone*. Everyone falls in love with her. Everyone reads one of her books and wants to know this woman personally. Everyone, upon meeting her or hearing her talk onstage, feels that sweet sense of connection, where it seems that she is sharing from her plainest, deepest self, and seeing into yours, and seeing who you are, and loving that, as is, without needing to change you, or fix you, or set you straight. She's the world's soul mate. She is best friends with Jesus, so she shares from abundance, and lives from her core, of tenderness and humor and curiosity. She just wants to share her amazement and gratitude for Christ's love, and the light with which He imbues our earth and our lives.

Of course, when I first realized that she has this effect on everyone, I grew bitter. But only for a few minutes. The truth is that

I do get to have Luci as my soul mate in this life, and that a person can't be with Luci or read her work without feeling immersed in matters of the soul: our joys and sorrow; our opportunities to live big and wild and alive; our freedom; our salvation.

—*Anne Lamott*

{ INTRODUCTION }

Start with What You Know

It was a long time before I figured this out.

When I was a child, growing up with my two brothers (one about a year older than I and the other two years younger), our mother had a way of giving us specific instructions that enabled her to get things done and encouraged us to live a certain way. I don't believe she was aware of it at the time, but as I've become a full-fledged adult and thought back on the things she wanted us to do or ways she wanted us to be, I've come to realize that Mother spoke to us more often than not in five-word sentences, always starting with a verb. Since the verb is the part of speech that requires action (and that's what Mother wanted), that verb held the key to making her desires known, so we'd get on with it—make tracks, do our chores, think right thoughts, behave in the manner she asked of us. And note that the verb had to be imperative because Mother was expressing a command or request.

For example, as children, when the boys were quiet (too quiet, according to Mother's antenna), she would say to me in all seriousness, "Go look for the boys," and just as I would take the first step to begin my search, she'd continue over her shoulder, "Tell 'em to quit it." It didn't matter what they were doing. The very notion that they were too quiet caused Mother to believe things were amiss, and she wanted me to check it out. (More often than not, they were wrestling or, as Mother would say, "rasslin'.")

As I grew a bit older, I'd often complain to Mother that I was bored. I wanted something to do but didn't know what. Very lovingly, she'd say, "Make something with your hands," and to this day that's one of my favorite things in life—inventing handmade things. Years later, as a college student packing for school, when I wasn't sure what to take, Mother said, "Start with what you know." And I now use that as a guideline for almost every undertaking: saving money, building a house, making a decision, or writing a book.

It's strange how one can go through the major part of life and not see certain patterns that have evolved through years of simply living. Then, when we're virtually "over the hill," it hits us out of the blue. That's what happened to me a couple of years ago, and it's out of those learned patterns that I'm writing this book. I've looked back over the various decades I've lived, loved, lost, learned, languished, and laughed and have compiled fifty simple chapters, sorted into five parts, that I trust will be helpful to you. I certainly don't know all the answers to a happy life, but I can tell you for a fact that there are a few simple secrets. Once we become acquainted with those, life is a lot richer and more fun.

Every chapter title starts with an imperative verb and is five words long. It's a simple premise that I trust will be easy to read and apply in your life. I'm suggesting we start with what we know. Then, as we move along we'll finally come to the chapter on living with an attitude of gratitude, no matter our circumstances. Basically, life is what we make it: the risks we take, the people we love, the battles we survive, the joys we share, and the instructions we take to heart. As Ralph Waldo Emerson said: "Life is a series of lessons which must be lived in order to be understood."

{ PART ONE }

Beginning
with the Basics

ONE

Honor Your Father and Mother

Most of us know it by heart even if we can't remember where we first heard it. It's the beginning of the fifth commandment listed in Exodus 20. You may have learned it as a child, but knowing this verse from memory and practicing it are two different things. Yet it's a basic tenet when it comes to enjoying a happy life. Interestingly, the commandment is to children, not parents, and since we are all children of parents, this verse applies to every one of us.

Initially, I interpreted the verse to mean "respect your mom and dad," but I now realize that *showing honor* to them is much weightier than *respect*. The word in the original Hebrew language meant "to be heavy, rich, honorable, and glorious," and it was most commonly used in reference to God's glory. Therefore, to give one's father and mother honor is to say that we (the children) understand the weighty responsibilities that come with parenting.

The apostle Paul repeats this commandment in Ephesians 6:2 and 3: "Honor your father and mother (which is the first commandment with a promise) so that it may be well with you, and that you may live long on the earth" (NASB). And the Greek word for *honor* here means "to show high regard for; to revere." I find that very thought provoking and have come to understand there are several reasons why this powerful instruction is one of the Ten Commandments.

First of all, this commandment upholds the principle of authority, without which we would not have a society that works. The first time a child sees authority is in the home, and if this authority is negated or neglected, the child will likely grow up to be irresponsible—and irresponsibility leads to a chaotic life and society.

Second, let's say you had very little love for your parents when you were growing up. Loving someone is not the same as giving them honor. All *honor* asks is to respect the position parents hold even if we don't like their personalities, lifestyles, or politics. It's similar to respecting the president of the United States simply because of the office he or she holds. The position itself commands honor.

And third, when there is honor on the part of the offspring, that honor will manifest itself in actions that protect, give care and goodness, exhibit generosity, and go the extra mile even though there may be no reciprocity on the part of the parent. In other words, when your parents grow older and cannot take care of themselves, you (as their child) will honor them by seeing that they are taken care of in a manner that is safe and healthy. Even if your parents are unbelievers, it's possible when you honor them in this manner that a door into their hearts will open to God because of your kindness and desire to regard them highly.

I have a dear friend who is a believer. She's an only child and her mother is a reprobate in every sense of the word and a rank *un*believer. To my knowledge, she's never taken personal responsibility for her daughter, herself, or anyone else. Ever. She's currently living in a care facility. Nevertheless, my friend has not missed a moment of seeing after her mother's needs in her old age. That is honoring to her mother, even though they couldn't be further apart in their beliefs and lifestyles. The daughter cares for her mother out of obedience to God. She's created careful and wise boundaries around the care she provides, doing what her mother needs without permitting her to control the money, time, or relationship.

In so many ways, I see God's provision for them both. As my friend cares for her mother, God cares for my friend and it "goes well with her," although it can be painful and confusing at times. I believe it's very possible, through my friend's kindness, that her mother may ultimately see her need for God and invite Christ into her heart. Who's to say? God works in mysterious ways to bring us into his kingdom. Anything is possible.

❧ TWO ❧

Be On Time for Everything

When I graduated from college in the spring of 1955, I went to work at an orphans' home, teaching water sports in the summer and art in the fall. Most of the teachers were still wet behind the ears from graduation, but we became good friends since we all lived in a nearby apartment house affiliated with the school. It was a fun time in life when each of us was just getting our moorings regarding careers and how they might play out in the future. There was always lots of input from everybody. We had the world by the tail and were ready to answer all questions when asked.

One evening Beverly, the music teacher, and I were casually chatting when she threw out an invitation for me to come to breakfast in her apartment the following Saturday. Beverly said something like, "Come to my house, and I'll make you a fancy breakfast."

Without giving it much thought, I responded, "Sure," never really intending to go—or not go. The invitation went in one ear and out the other. So on Saturday, when it wasn't all that convenient for me to actually get there for breakfast, I just stayed home. Later in the day I dropped by Beverly's place, and when she answered the door I could see she'd been crying.

"Where've you been, Luci?" she asked. She proceeded to tell me she'd prepared a gourmet recipe that morning, something she thought I would especially like, and all week she had been looking forward to our time together. When I didn't come, she wondered if I'd gotten sick or been hurt or had just forgotten about it. Embarrassed and chagrined, I apologized. Then I confessed that I remembered her invitation but simply hadn't taken it seriously. I was in the wrong. She accepted my apology and was kind in her response, but I could tell she was very hurt.

That experience taught me a huge lesson about keeping my word. I knew better than to just not show up. After all, my father had always insisted his children be prompt, courteous, and on time for everything. But for some reason, it hadn't seemed to matter that day. The thought that has really stuck with me through the years, though, was Beverly's question, "Where've you been, Luci?"

It made me realize how important it is to pay attention. It taught me to listen to what is being said and how I'm responding. If I'm not serious or paying attention, even in a casual conversation, it's not fair to the other person—who might just be inviting me to do something fun or interesting! I never want to disappoint someone again the way I disappointed Beverly, and I don't want them to wait on me, wondering, *She said she was coming . . . but is she?*

To help ensure that I'm on time for everything to which I've committed, I make it a habit to listen, to be focused in a personal conversation, to really hear another's words, to clarify when I don't understand, and to fully engage in whatever I'm doing and whoever is with me. Always. All the time.

Eventually, what started as a conscious effort has become a natural pattern and a personal habit; today it serves as a corollary secret that helps me be on time for everything. Focusing firmly on what's being said to me isn't always easy, but it's always kind.

Here's my A-list for being fully present in a conversation:

- Be sure I listen.
- Be sure I understand what's being communicated.
- Be sure I'm clear about what's involved before I commit to something.
- Be sure I can do what I say I will do.
- Be sure I show up on time!

I remember this list because it started with Beverly, a name that begins with a *B*, and that reminds me of the word *be*. That little verb carries a lot of weight. *Be* has movement in it. It means being alive, inside and out. But it's up to us as to *how* alive we want to be—how responsible, how engaged, and, ultimately, how trustworthy.

Shakespeare got it right: "To be or not to be: That is the question." One of the simple secrets of a happy life is *to be* on time for everything.

{ THREE }

Take Jesus with You Everywhere

I can hardly remember a day in my childhood when my mother wasn't somewhere in the house singing. She had a beautiful soprano voice and would spontaneously break into song. Not only would she sing, but also on occasion she'd dance down the hallway to music on the radio or grab the broom and waltz with it as her partner around the kitchen. Sometimes as she sang she would motion for one of us kids to add harmony. She knew many hymns by heart and sang them frequently and heartily as she did her chores or cooked a meal.

I well remember a favorite of hers was an old hymn called "Take the Name of Jesus with You." Mother believed every word she sang:

Take the name of Jesus with you,
Child of sorrow and of woe;
It will joy and comfort give you—
Take it, then, wher-e'er you go.

Precious name, O how sweet!
Hope of earth and joy of heav'n,
Precious name, O how sweet!
Hope of earth and joy of heav'n.

Interestingly, just writing those words forms a picture in my mind of something that happened more than sixty years ago. I can see it clearly in my head. I remember leaving for school with Mother singing that at the kitchen sink, and when I said goodbye, she looked over her shoulder and said, "Take Jesus with you today, honey."

I knew instinctively that Mother wanted to assure me Jesus would be with me regardless of what happened that day for good or bad. He would be in my thoughts and actions—with me on my walk to school, down the hallways, in my classrooms, when I talked with my friends, or answered questions from the teacher. He'd be with me on the court when I played volleyball after school or met with the swim team. And Mother wanted me to know that on my way home, Jesus would go before me, protecting me and bringing me home safely. She didn't want me to spend a minute of the day without the consciousness of his presence. Although I was walking out the door that morning, I was not alone. I was never alone.

Now that I look back over many years of living, I can tell you it's one of the best lessons Mother ever taught me. She had no idea when she casually threw that phrase over her shoulder what a valuable tool she was giving me.

Or maybe she did.

Trusting that God was with her (and with her family) seemed second nature to Mother. She was a student of his Word and rested in his faithfulness. She didn't worry, fret, or fear. She believed God and knew he could be trusted completely. She didn't just "preach" it, she lived it and sang of it with confidence. What I first saw in my mother, I came to experience on my own; I don't struggle with the sovereignty of God or his faithfulness, and I've never seen doubt in either of my brothers. How do I explain it? There may be many reasons, but certainly one is the assurance of faith in God that our mother demonstrated, both in her words and her example. She reflected the truth of Colossians 3:16 and 17:

> Let the word of Christ—the Message—have the run of the house. Give it plenty of room in your lives. Instruct and direct one another using good common sense. And sing, sing your hearts out to God! Let every detail in your lives—words, actions, whatever—be done in the name of the Master, Jesus, thanking God the Father every step of the way.

{ FOUR }

Let People Know You Care

Several months ago, Mary Graham and I were talking about kindness, having a tender spirit, and caring about other people, and I asked her to tell me the most caring individual she's ever encountered in life. Since Mary's in her sixties and has lived a long, full life of reaching out to thousands of people all over the world through Campus Crusade and now as the president of Women of Faith, I could hardly wait for her answer. After a couple of minutes she said, "I'd have to say Thidwick."

"Who?"

"*Thidwick, the Big-hearted Moose* by Dr. Seuss."

"You've gotta be kiddin' me! There's a moose named Thidwick?"

"Yes! Dr. Seuss wrote a book about him sixty years ago. I memorized it when I was a freshman in high school. It's a poem that tells the story of Thidwick letting all these little animals live in his antlers for free. There's a bug, a spider, a couple of birds, four squirrels, a bobcat, a turtle, on and on. Even a fox, a big bear, and a whole swarm of bees. Thidwick had such a big heart he couldn't say no, so everybody moved in and took over. I've quoted that poem to all my nieces and nephews through the years as I babysat them because it has such a good moral—although in the end, Thidwick took the concept a little too far."

I loved the fact Mary knew that book and answered my question with a moose. (Never look a gift-moose in the mouth!) Being generous, softhearted, and sweet to others is almost a lost art in today's world. Even though there are lots of Scriptures that make reference to caring, it takes time to care, and few people want to give that kind of time. Matthew 5:7 says, "You're blessed when you care." And in 1 Corinthians 13 we're reminded, "Love cares more for others than for self."

But the story of Thidwick teaches another truth about caring that might be more important and leads to an even happier life. It's learning how to say no to those who want to take advantage of us when we care. The bevy of animals living in Thidwick's antlers wanted too much. They called the shots, told him where to go and what to do, and invited more "guests" to live with them.

Some of us are like that. We move in and invite others to come along. Or we allow others to move in and invite guests.

Where's the balance between caring and being careful? Where's the boundary line? As caring people, when we let others run over us and take advantage of us, we're in a pickle before we know it. That's what happened to Thidwick:

> *You couldn't say "Skat!" 'cause that wouldn't be right.*
> *You couldn't shout "Scram!" 'cause that isn't polite.*

So when should a boundary line be drawn? When the degree of caring negatively affects our quality of life and inadvertently invites carelessness on the part of the other person. Dr. Seuss himself once said, "Unless someone like you cares a whole awful lot, nothing is going to get better."

That's true, but as he beautifully illustrated in the life of Thidwick, balance is required. In order to do the two simultaneously (and it *can* be done), we need to turn the whole ball of wax over to God, who gives us balance. For guidance, look to the promise in Psalm 91:14–15: "I'll give you the best of care if you'll only get to know and trust me. Call me and I'll answer, be at your side in bad times; I'll rescue you, then throw you a party."

As Christians, we're to show kindness to others and care for them. But while God's Word teaches us to put others' needs before our own, it also reminds us to care for ourselves as well—as his cherished children whom he created with love. That means striking a balance as we care—with caution.

{ FIVE }

Learn to Organize Your Stuff

If your stuff isn't organized, it has the potential to drive you crazy. For me, I simply can't concentrate when things are out of whack: my files are a mess, my closet's in chaos, or dirty dishes wait in the sink. I may try to ignore out-of-place things, but they're so distracting. All I can think about is straightening things up. Call me crazy, but it's the truth. People often ask how I manage to keep "order in my court." If you're one of those people, here are half a dozen ideas that might help:

1. Decide what you want organized and find time to do it.
Take time to figure out what's important to keep—and what can be stored or given away. Start there. Don't rush.

Look through what you've treasured all these years and make sure it's still important in your life. Even if this chore takes weeks or months to finish, it'll be worth the effort. If you decide to keep it, find a place for it right there and then. Don't put it off.

2. *Make lists and follow them carefully, marking off what gets done.*

Lists keep you on track and your sanity intact in this chaotic world. Write down where you put things, what you want to keep, and what means something to you. You can store the list in your iPhone or BlackBerry, but write it down somewhere. In a busy life, how do we remember things without lists?

3. *Clean up smaller areas first to give yourself a sense of accomplishment.*

This is by far one of my favorite ways to organize, and even more so as I get older. Here's why: little by little it all gets done. And what doesn't get done probably wasn't that important anyway. When we look too far ahead, it's discouraging. So work awhile and then stop and savor your small accomplishment.

4. *Create a place for specific things and return them there after using them.*

Let's say your jewelry drawer is a mess. Buy plastic boxes with compartments and separate the gold from the silver or handmade from machine made or sort any other way that makes sense to you. Put your jewelry in those boxes, and put the boxes back in the drawer. When you wear a pair of earrings, put them back where they go when you take them off. The same goes for books, CDs, photographs, letters—whatever. If it's important to you, give it a spot to call its own.

5. *Forgive yourself for days you're not organized, but don't get used to that state.*

Since you're a human being in a broken world, you're not going to be organized every day of your life. Give yourself grace. It's like riding a bicycle. Even if you fall off, you never think, *Well, this just doesn't work for me. I'll never try it again.* You get back on track, knowing it's all part of the process. Keep going, and in time, you'll fall less and less.

Here's the point: if we get low and stay there, we'll never get organized because the fun of accomplishment will get buried under the burden of procrastination or depression.

6. *Celebrate and rejoice over the messes you've straightened up.*

I'm a big fan of having fun as I go along in life. Without parties or shouting or dancing or visiting or laughing now and then, life is too hard. After cleaning up a mess, invite friends or family over to see what you've done. Take pictures of "before" and "after" and stick them in your journal, your Bible, or on the mirror. Cleaning up something is a huge reason to throw a party. When I have a big project to organize, I put on great music and whistle or dance while I work.

Here's the biblical encouragement to being organized: "Be sure that everything is done properly and in order" (1 Corinthians 14:40 NLT). Not only that, but the Bible even specifies paying taxes as a step toward living an organized life. Look at Romans 13:5–6, which says, "You must live responsibly—not just to avoid punishment but also because it's the right way to live. That's also why you pay taxes—so that an orderly way of life can be maintained."

SIX

Keep Your Word Every Time

Keeping your word every time depends upon the amount of integrity you have within yourself—and integrity is a two-sided coin: one side reflects the respect you have toward another individual, and the other side shows how much you respect yourself. The two sides are reflected in Jesus's words in Luke 6:31: "Do to others as you would have them do to you" (NIV).

Keeping your word means you're going to do what you say you'll do. And isn't that what we want of others too? If a friend or business contact promises to do something, we want him or her to keep that promise.

The importance of being a woman of my word was confirmed for me when, after I had worked for twenty years as a draftsman-artist with Mobil Oil Corporation (long before it became Exxon Mobil), I was promoted to an executive position as manager of rights of way and claims for their West Coast pipeline division. While I was honored and thrilled about this offer, I have to admit I also was scared to death of what a job of that magnitude would entail.

Could I do it? Did I have the brains to run a division? Was I qualified enough to make decisions that would affect the entire company, not just my own standards?

I knew I was a good employee because there's no way I could have been given that opportunity had I not demonstrated years of punctuality and dedication. But an executive? That was a whole new ballgame.

As I was contemplating Mobil's offer, I decided to phone my friend Martha, a public relations professional, and ask her opinion of my taking the new job. Martha was a seasoned Mobil employee whose life showed a great deal of integrity. I trusted her judgment and knew she'd give me an honest response.

She listened as I laid out the situation, and then she enthusiastically encouraged me to take the job. "It's right up your alley," she said. "You enjoy people, you're a hard worker, you're not afraid of change, you love a challenge, and you'll be the first woman in a management position in that division. Do it!" Then she added this clincher: "Just remember two things: don't be afraid to ask questions, and never sign anything until you're sure."

I've never been shy about asking questions, so that was a no-brainer. It was the second part of Martha's advice that resonated within me: *never sign anything until you're sure.* She was reminding me that when I signed something, I would be giving my word. I would be saying, "Yes, I will do this." Or in this case, "I will see that my company does this." I needed to be sure I understood what I was promising so that I made good on that promise every time.

It all sounded a lot like my own philosophy that I'd lived by all my adult life: "Say what you mean and *do* what you say."

Putting all those thoughts together, I felt a surge of confidence, knowing *I can do this job*.

And I did. That job opened a whole new world to me, both in my work life and in my personal life. I loved it! But whenever a contract or agreement was to be finalized, I made sure I understood everything involved because I was giving my word, and I wanted to keep my word every time.

Even today, long retired, I am very cautious before I sign a document of any sort. I read it thoroughly and determine if I fully understand and trust it before I sign my name. After all, it's my name that gives credence to the agreement. If I sign it, that means I will keep my word.

You won't be surprised to read the source of this simple but powerful secret. It's right there in Psalm 15:5: "Keep your word even when it costs you, make an honest living, never take a bribe. You'll never get blacklisted if you live like this."

SEVEN

Make Something with Your Hands

If I remember correctly, it started in the sixth grade. For Christmas that year, I got a set of Lincoln Logs, one of the best gifts I've ever received. From those logs I built bridges, buildings, and roadways. I was in heaven!

Seeing my dedication to Lincoln Logs, my family and friends gave me paint sets, model airplanes and ships, Legos, scrapbooks, and reams of paper I could make into kites or use for drawing. Making something with my hands was a fascinating way to grow up. And I still feel that way today—sixty-eight years after my first set of Lincoln Logs.

What is it about handmade things that gives me such a thrill?

First, I love the sense of accomplishment, and nothing provides that satisfaction like making something with my hands.

Second, it's a challenge. I want to see if I can do it.

Third, I enjoy figuring things out . . . feeling the thrill of knowing how parts come together to move or squeak or react.

Would you believe that a few years ago, three different friends gave me the *same* book for my birthday: *The Way Things Work* by David Macaulay? I've read it from cover to cover and *love* that book. (And for Christmas that same year, I was given two copies of *The Way Things Really Work*.)

I'd give anything to take off a whole year and do nothing but make gifts so that every time I handed a friend or family member a present, it'd be one I'd made. Oh, gosh! I'd love that. Maybe that idea comes from an incident many years ago when I gave my friend Ruth a birthday present and the moment she received it, she said very sincerely, "Did you make this, Luci?"

I replied, "What if I didn't?"

With all the seriousness in the world, and knowing full well I hadn't made it, she said, "I'll give you another chance."

My mother taught me to make things, and she was a fabulous teacher: artistic, thorough, fun, and extremely creative. Mother had a reputation for making everything. I was standing by her in church one Sunday when a woman next to her told Mother how much she loved the perfume she was wearing. "I'll bet you made it, didn't you?"

Our family got a good laugh out of that, not only because it was such a telling question but because there was enough truth to it that Mother *could* have made it, had she set her mind to it.

And my father was a fabulous builder of things and teacher as well: patient, experimental, clever, and encouraging. He'd draw cartoons on a little pad and then would ask me to draw one. He lettered beautifully and taught me how to do it before I ever entered the first grade. To this day, I print notes all the time rather than write them in cursive.

My dad also gave me my first little toolbox—to match his big one. Again, I was in heaven. Together, Daddy and I repaired clocks, toilets, garage doors, skates, and various gadgets around the house.

In 1983 the very first message I gave publicly as a professional was about a young man who (with a friend) made something with his hands in his parents' garage. That man was the late Steve Jobs, and that something was the first Apple computer. Look where that design took him.

And what about God? Look at what *he* made by hand: everything! And he's the ultimate teacher. His creativity is limitless. Isaiah 48:13 tells us, "Earth is my work, handmade. And the skies— I made them, too, horizon to horizon. When I speak, they're on their feet, at attention."

We have no way of knowing what God has in store for us if we simply use our hands to plant ideas and dreams and then watch them take root.

{ EIGHT }

Do All Your Homework First

Did you know there's actually a website called Cramster.com? At this site you can insert any question about your homework and it'll give you the answer. Honestly!

You might be thinking, *I wish I'd known that a long time ago when I was* . . . Not I. Even as a child in school, there would've been no temptation for me to bypass homework. I loved it. I'm not kidding. I had a passion to learn, research, read, write, and study. It was in my DNA. I'd start the minute I got home from school and not move until it was completely finished.

While I loved learning, then and now, my enjoyment of homework was more than that. As a child, I was primarily motivated just to get it done. Why? Because it was there. Even now, when I have something to do, I can hardly rest until it's done. I love to play, putter, visit, travel, and enjoy a thousand things in life, but when something needs to be finalized, I want to get at it. I'm what my brothers call "a finisher." Friends teasingly say to me that finishing is my favorite feeling because my life is so ordered by discipline. They say I have an overactive responsibility gland. Maybe I do, but whatever it is, finishing something brings me a lot of satisfaction.

That kind of discipline began in grade school. If I remember correctly, it started with doing homework because I dived into it the minute I got in the door.

I'm so grateful my study habits were established and well developed back then, because *now* I'm never late for a meeting, an appointment, a flight, a payment, or a deadline. Somehow, I've always known that life's responsibilities don't manage themselves, so if we're not intentional, we can end up disordered, disarrayed, disappointed, and discontent.

People often ask me how I happen to be so organized. Seriously, I think it's because I started so young and stayed at it—until as recently as this morning. I love the feeling of accomplishment, and I love being responsible. My parents instilled that in me and honored the trait as it developed in me. I thrived in that environment.

Basically, school homework teaches us two things—discipline and development—and we'll be dealing with these things as long as we live. Don't ask me how I know this; just trust me that I do.

For instance, take discipline, which has to do with obedience and training. If we do something often enough, it becomes a habit. It makes for an orderly life. Not boring—orderly. When we come home from school and do homework as soon as possible, we're extending the mind-set we've already established in school.

I'm not saying it will help us make better grades. (More often than not, both of my brothers made better grades than I.) But I am saying that having the responsibility for finishing homework right after school when we're young helps us find discipline for life when we're older. Discipline is a choice, not a feeling, and we're never too old to choose to do the right thing.

And then, development: Once we're in the habit of doing what's right, discipline becomes part of our nature. If we do that long enough, it actually develops into a way of life. And, more often than not, it brings out the capabilities and possibilities of a better life. I believe that to have a rich, meaningful, enjoyable, and happy life, one has to have self-control and initiative. Those traits come with discipline, and discipline leads to development.

I think it'd be interesting to ask Cramster.com how one can develop the fine art of discipline, don't you? Who knows? The answer might be: do your homework first.

{ NINE }

Treat Other People with Kindness

A number of years ago I was standing out in front of the car wash in my neighborhood in California, idly watching traffic in the thoroughfare while waiting for my car to be serviced, wiped down, and detailed, when a beat-up, dirty old SUV pulled into the driveway, driven by a guy who hadn't shaved in weeks, hadn't had a haircut in months, and was totally unkempt in every sense of the word. In the backseats of his Land Rover were five kids, all looking pretty much like the driver (only without beards). There were three boys and two girls ranging in ages from about four to ten or eleven. It's hard to see that many children (especially with a man) and not have your attention completely captured.

When the SUV stopped, the driver got out and walked around behind it, opened the back and began taking the kids out of the car one by one. I carefully watched this whole procedure and was utterly amazed at this guy and his children. Every one of them called him "Daddy," and I never in my life saw a person kinder than he. He cuddled the little ones as they laughed and kissed him on the cheek. And the older children teased and giggled and were exceedingly obedient. I stood there enchanted by their interaction. It melted my heart, and my first thought was, *Don't judge a book by its cover, Luci*—a lesson I'd learned from my father as a child.

After a bit, when all the children were out of the car, they sat by one another on a long bench, with each of them wanting "the best seat" next to their dad. The SUV had moved into the car-wash area by this time, and while the family waited, they all began to sing a little ditty they'd memorized. Never once did the father raise his hand or his voice. He was so gentle with those kids, yet he kept them in line by being totally present and engaged with each child. And his engagement overflowed to their interaction with one another. They were what we used to call a happy family.

I'll never forget that scene. It captured a place in my heart forever. I was mesmerized by how the dad treated those kids. And his kindness to them must have been contagious because they were so thoughtful and sweet to each other. When do you see that kind of behavior in public?

My favorite attribute in people is kindness. It melts me every time, and I do find it contagious. I like seeing it more than humility, compassion, forgiveness, self-control, or even (spare me if this is your favorite) love. While I recognize all these characteristics come from God and I'm everlastingly grateful they're ours by virtue of a relationship with Christ, kindness still wins my heart, hands down!

Kindness embodies so many of those other attributes because it's a compilation that's experienced (and seen) in one's attitude toward other people. It's a package deal.

God is kindness personified. In 1 Peter 2:3, we're invited to "drink deep of God's pure kindness. Then you'll grow up mature and whole in God." That's quite a statement. What Christian doesn't want to be "mature and whole in God"? We get that way by seeing and recognizing God's kindness to us and then passing it on.

Remembering that little family at the car wash makes me think of another verse, Ephesians 4:32: "Be kind and compassionate to one another, forgiving each other, just as in Christ God forgave you" (NIV). Watching those kids and their dad show kindness to one another was a great incentive for me to be kind to everybody I meet—and I still am reminded of that incentive by the memory. Kindness is a gift to receive and a joy to give.

{ TEN }

Read Your Bible
Every Day

Aristotle once wrote, "Good habits formed at youth make all the difference." But what if we start good habits once we're past youth? Will they still make a difference?

I think they will. It's never too late to start a good habit. Take Bible reading, for example. Reading your Bible every day is a bit like reading a weight scale. Most of us have bathroom scales in our home, so we're familiar with the process of weighing ourselves. There are two things we need in order to weigh: a private place and a scale. How simple is that?

And if we mean business, we follow certain guidelines. For instance, we might:

- Weigh at the same time every day.
- Remove our clothing and shoes.
- Step on the scale.
- Focus on the process without getting hung up on the weight.

In the same way, we need two things to get started with daily Bible reading: a private place and a Bible. And if we mean business, we may follow certain guidelines. For instance, we might:

- Read at the same time every day.
- Set aside the things in our lives that would distract.
- Open the Bible.
- Focus on reading the words without getting hung up on what weighs us down.

This simple system motivates us while helping us avoid discouragement that can come when we get bogged down. Reading God's Word takes time, but if we keep in mind that it's much like weighing ourselves every day, the discipline of it makes it achievable. Without having a program or a plan, it's easy to let Bible reading get lost in the shuffle of our busy days. And ultimately our spiritual health suffers as a result.

Someone once asked a great Shakespearean scholar, "How do you study Shakespeare?"

His response was very clear: *"Read* Shakespeare."

Studying the Bible is the same. You read it, and as you read, you become acquainted with its precepts, promises, power, and the Person of God the Father, his Son, and the Holy Spirit.

The Bible is the bedrock of truth, and in it are the words of life, so there are understandable reasons to read it daily. I hardly remember a day in my growing-up years when I didn't see my mother reading her Bible. Sitting in her bed, on the sofa, at the dining table, or on the front porch, she'd have her Bible open, reading it every single day. Rare were the times she told *me* to read it. But by modeling Bible reading, the message was perhaps stronger. It's a vivid picture in my mind.

Mother often copied verses on three-by-five cards and tucked them here and there around the house where she could see them and meditate on them throughout the day. She didn't want to miss what God said to her and what he wanted to do in her life. Those verses were both life giving and life changing. Nothing influenced the life of my siblings and me more than our mother's consistency in reading the Word of God.

I now have—and treasure—the Bible Mother loved and read daily until she died in 1971. It's filled with her markings and notes, and it's held together by tape. Right in front, in Mother's inimitable handwriting, are these words, written along with the verse I've quoted in this book's dedication. I don't know if they're her words or if they're something she heard and loved in her Bible class: "The Word of God reveals the righteousness of God and the sinfulness of man. It reveals the plan of God about salvation to unbelievers and the way of life for believers in any age."

Because Mother believed and lived out that truth on a consistent basis, she made me want to read the Bible daily as well. Frankly, I like it much better than stepping on those scales every morning.

{ **PART TWO** }

Developing Your Style

{ ELEVEN }

Draw a Picture to Understand

Years ago, I had an art teacher who loved birds. She drew them every chance she got. During the time she was my professor, she found a dead duck and took it home to study. She especially wanted to know how the wings worked and made drawing after drawing as she tried to figure it out. She looked at all of the feathers under a blow dryer, studying how they might move in flight.

Don't you love that? She wanted to understand ducks, to satisfy her curiosity.

The key word in this secret is *understand*. Of course, in today's world with so many electronic gadgets, you may think you don't need to put pencil to paper and literally draw something to understand it.

But I believe making a drawing, even a rudimentary one, can help you get a more detailed picture of what you see. And you don't have to be a great artist.

This secret was reinforced for me in May 1999, when three friends and I went to Africa on safari. We each took a small walkie-talkie so we could talk about what we were seeing without yelling when we ended up in different groups. I wanted to make sure I would be able to use it easily and quickly, so I made a drawing in my travel journal with all the parts labeled: talk button, monitor control, microphone, on/off switch, volume control, antenna— the whole nine yards. Having done that, I became familiar with the device and comfortable using it at the drop of a hat. Because I understood how to work it, when two of my travel companions were on a "walking safari," the other two of us could enjoy their excited reports every ten or fifteen minutes, keeping us up-to-date on what was happening: "Baby giraffe, twelve o'clock," or "We're looking straight into the eyes of a bush buck," or "We're lying on the ground to avoid a swarm of bees."

Seeing the drawing of the walkie-talkie in my journal helps me even now, letting me enjoy that sweet memory to this day.

And then, there was the time I had an inner ear infection. In my desire to understand exactly what was going on in my sore ear (after the doctor had explained it to me), I looked it up in a medical book and made a drawing of it in my journal. Several years later, when I had the same kind of infection, I went to an ear-nose-throat doctor, who confirmed that I had correctly diagnosed my own problem because of that earlier drawing.

Actually, to draw is part of being me. I'm not the artist I'd like to be, but being able to sketch helps me understand various things in life that interest me. Not only do I draw to understand, but also for my own pleasure. It's my style.

During the early 1970s I spent many summer vacations in Greece with my friend Sophia, who lived in Athens. One year, instead of going to a Greek island, as we had done before, she suggested we go to Arachova, a little town on the mountainside of Parnassus that is famous for its beautiful woven items. Since I was doing a lot of weaving back then, I loved the idea. We rented a Volkswagen and started out. On the way, Sophia thought it'd be fun to ride donkeys up Mount Parnassus, just to see everything from another perspective. When we came to a place called Donkey Stop, we left the car there and each got on a donkey.

With a ballpoint pen, I drew on the leg of my blue jeans as we rode along, noting a little car, the donkey stop, various trees, and a stream we crossed. When we stopped to look at the scenery—houses picturesquely spilling down the mountainside—and take a few photos, we decided to have a little picnic right there. It was fun . . . until we got ready to leave and realized we were completely turned around and didn't know which way to go! Fortunately, by consulting my "leg map" we could look for a stream (the one we had crossed getting there) and then the trees and then the donkey stop and the little car, and we managed to retrace our steps back to our beginning spot, laughing all the way.

Drawing pictures not only satisfies my curiosity, it also helps me understand the things I use, the places I go—and the adventures (and sometimes the misadventures) I enjoy. Try it, and you'll see what I mean.

{ TWELVE }

Accept Events As They Happen

I don't panic. Ever. I'm exceedingly calm in a storm and have been that way all my life. I'm like my father. My mother was "a balloon on a string," but Daddy? Cool as a cucumber. Really.

It was amazing to watch. One of my oldest memories occurred when I was about seven and we lived in Fort Worth. Someone in the house (I say it was one of my brothers; they say it was me) had accidentally left the water running in the bathtub with the stopper in it and then joined the family to go visit our cousins. When we got home, water was all over the house. Mother was sick at heart and could hardly believe her eyes. She went into the kitchen and cried, but my brothers and I thought it was one of the coolest things we'd ever witnessed. Daddy, calm as could be, assigned us various rooms to mop up, and within an hour, we had moved furniture, dried the floor, wrung out a dozen soaked towels, and sat down to steaming cups of hot chocolate Mother had made for us while wading around in the kitchen. It was an adventure.

Like Daddy, I'm calm in emergencies. But don't talk to me about interruptions! Or delays. I hate those and could write a book about why they drive me nuts. Delayed flights, long waits at the doctor's office, and s-l-o-w drivers in the fast lane challenge me. I have to remind myself to breathe.

Accepting events as they happen—good or bad, hard or easy, horrific tragedies or mere inconveniences, our fault or not—is often very difficult to do. It requires the ability to get outside ourselves, look at the big picture, and rely on the sovereignty of God. In his second letter to his friend Timothy, the apostle Paul gave Timothy (and us) guidelines on how to do just that: "But you—keep your eye on what you're doing; accept the hard times along with the good; keep the Message alive; do a thorough job as God's servant" (2 Timothy 4:5).

Not long ago, a Florida friend and I decided that would be "our verse" for the year. We found it at the same time in our Bible reading, loved it, and chose it as a great verse for our lives. To me, the most difficult part of it is accepting the hard times along with the good because I know that, for me, "hard times" include interruptions and delays. If it's just inconveniences, I can manage, but to be detained . . . that's another story.

But I finally figured this out: to "accept the hard times along with the good," I need to apply the context of the rest of the verse. In order to "accept" I have to:

- Keep my eye on what I'm doing (no matter what).
- Keep God's Word alive in my heart and behavior.
- Keep being God's servant to other people.

When I do that and stay at it, I have a much easier time accepting events as they happen.

I had occasion to put that reasoning to the test recently when a friend called me while I was knee deep in writing. I desperately wanted to get on paper what I was thinking for the next paragraph before I forgot it, so I had little or no interest in listening.

I could feel myself losing patience, when all of a sudden "my verse" hit me. Under my breath, I asked the Lord to calm my spirit, to help me listen carefully to what was being said, and to remember I was here to serve my friend, not to finish my paragraph.

Meanwhile, he went on and on about the burdens he was facing and how sad they made him feel.

I listened.

Then, after a bit, he told me how much it helped him just to talk about what he was going through and how much he appreciated my time. His circumstance hadn't changed, but his spirit had.

When I hung up, I finished writing the paragraph and found myself feeling glad my friend had called and grateful that I was able to help him. Then I again stopped writing and thanked God for that verse and that reminder.

{ THIRTEEN }

Stay Proactive About Your Health

It's been said that the human body, with proper care, will last a lifetime. Makes one wonder what constitutes "proper care." I think of the body as a home. It's your home because you live in it. Because you live in it, you want to protect it from intruders. It's an important investment and provides you shelter. Consider this:

- Your bones are the two-by-fours that support the structure.
- Your frame of mind is what gives you joy and peace.
- Your eyes are the windows; your lungs provide ventilation.
- Your heart is the water main, and your brain is the food processor.

- Your hair is the lawn, and your weight is more often than not that stuff in the attic you want to get rid of. The better you know things about your home, the easier it is to maintain it, decorate it, and enjoy it.

Using that analogy, let's look at your body as something that needs, from time to time, the same maintenance and repairs as your home. If your toilet won't stop running, for example, you don't call a plumber first thing. No, you take the top off the tank and fool around with the floating ball until the problem corrects itself. If a lightbulb burns out, you don't call an electrician. Nor do you call the pest-control guy when a fly lands on your kitchen counter. You rely on yourself to maintain control over simple issues that need attention. In short, you are proactive about what has to be done.

Our goal in life should be to maintain our bodies in such a way that we avoid things that cause the most wear and tear and seek things that provide the most value. But do we do that? Realistically, I don't think so. But I have found, in my seven decades of living, that the best health care is moderation. We ourselves can control a lot when it comes to the maintenance of our own bodies. And in many ways, that maintenance controls the destiny of our health.

I'm no expert on this topic, although I've almost always enjoyed amazingly good health. And because I've studied art all my life, I've had a keen fascination with the human body. It is nothing short of miraculous, a dynamic reflection of the genius of our Creator.

A couple years ago I bought a book that has helped me enormously with this whole subject. It's *YOU: The Owner's Manual* by Michael F. Roizen and Mehmet C. Oz. It's a guide to feeling healthier and younger. Initially I bought it because I loved the title and the very clear, clever, descriptive drawings and lettering throughout. But as I began to read it, I found it had the answers to many of the questions I was asking about how my body works.

However, there's an even better book that teaches us to be proactive about good health. It's the Bible. Look at the apostle Paul's words in Colossians 2:19: "The source of life, Christ, who puts us together in one piece, whose very breath and blood flow through us. He is the Head and we are the body. We can grow up healthy in God only as he nourishes us."

Last week I was in the doctor's office for my annual physical, and I overheard an elderly woman say to the desk person as she was leaving, "Good health doesn't just take care of itself, and it's most often lost by those of us who assume it will." She's right! The better our health, the more energy we have to enjoy life to the fullest.

{ FOURTEEN }

Value the Things You Have

When I was nine, my parents bought me a bicycle. I had no idea how to ride it, but that didn't stop me from climbing on and heading out. Somehow, I expected the bike to automatically do what I wanted it to. I assumed it would "mind me." (After all, my other toys seemed to.)

Of course, it didn't. I spent a lot of time falling, getting up, crying, and throwing it against a tree in the front yard. The girl next door also had a bike, and she could ride like a house afire. That's what I wanted to do. We kept telling each other we'd race one day, but how could I do that if I couldn't even stay up on the thing? It never occurred to me to ask for help in learning to ride the bicycle.

I was much too independent (or maybe stubborn?) for that. So I tossed the bike aside and tried to ignore it. It was of no value to me.

One evening I overheard my parents talking about the money they had spent on my bike. They weren't complaining; they were just trying to figure out how to help me enjoy their investment. It made me feel awful. My dad had carefully looked through the Sears and Roebuck Catalog to choose just the perfect bicycle for me: right weight, correct height, perfect wheel balance, name-brand company.

After eavesdropping on their conversation, I went into the room where Mother and Daddy were talking and told them how bad I felt about throwing my bike against the tree.

Ever the encourager, my dad said something like, "We understand, honey. We know you want to ride, and your bike just won't behave long enough for you to stay on it. Let me show you all the things that make this bike a wonderful machine. Maybe it'll help you figure it out."

Then he opened the catalog to the section on bicycles. He pointed out the one they had bought me and talked about all its features that help people become good bike riders.

Once I saw what went into that little two-wheeled beauty, my whole attitude changed—toward it and toward the skill of riding. I respected the bicycle and wanted to learn how to ride. The next morning, I went to the garage and apologized to the bike for throwing it around. I know this sounds a little strange to those of you who don't have a history of talking to inanimate objects, but that's what I did. I talked to my bike and told it that I now realized what a good bike it was, and I promised to be nicer to it in the future. If my daddy believed in it, and if he chose it especially for me, I wanted to believe in it too.

In his typical way, my father, full of kindness, had helped me appreciate the value of his and Mother's purchase. Somehow, his high regard for its quality made me want to appreciate the bike's impressive features too. With my dad's encouragement and my new attitude—a new determination—I quickly learned to ride the bicycle. From that day forward, it was a trusted companion and dependable mode of childhood transportation for me.

Since the bicycle, I've been cautious about what I've bought, and I've treated my possessions with great care. My home is filled with things I've purchased and gifts I've been given through the years. Some of them are almost as old as I am. I take great delight in being surrounded with stuff that has meaning for me. My friends tease me, but it seems like even the pots and pans have their own story.

Of course, valuing the things we're blessed to own and living for our possessions are two separate things. They are, after all, only *things*, and we don't want them to distract us from what's really important: living a life that's pleasing to God. Instead, as we enjoy and value the things we own, we need to simultaneously value the life God has given us, thanking him for gifts of friends and experiences.

Looking at my possessions brings back memories of yesteryear, of friends of long ago, of places I've visited on God's beautiful earth. These are the treasures in my house that reflect who I am. Without ever speaking, they tell the story of my life.

{ FIFTEEN }

Focus on What's Important *Now*

I woke up this morning, sneezing. Don't you hate it when that happens? Today had been set aside to write, and it's hard to concentrate when I have a cold. All morning I blew my nose, coughed, sneezed, and talked in the bass cleft. I felt lethargic, and the further I went into the day, the more lethargic I got. My phone rang, and when I answered, my neighbor said, "You don't sound like yourself."

"Oh, really?" I croaked. "I'm doing well to answer the phone, much less breathe. I think I have a cold."

She was very sympathetic and asked if she could take me to the doctor. That was the last thing I wanted to do. I shot back, "I don't have time for the doctor. I'm not going. I know this is just a little cold, and it'll pass."

"What's more important today than your health, Luci?" she asked.

When I told her I needed to work on chapter 15, she asked me the topic. I was hesitant to tell her it was "focus on what's important *now*," but when I did, she said, "Well, duh! Isn't your cold a perfect example of what you're writing? If you don't focus on getting rid of that cold, I'm afraid you're going to feel worse, and you won't be able to write at all this week. Think about it."

I did, and as I was thinking, I happened to remember back to my topic in chapter 13: "Stay Proactive About Your Health."

I decided to follow my friend's suggestion and go to the doctor. In fact, she drove me. Turns out I had a bronchial, upper respiratory infection that required a steroid shot and antibiotics to treat. My chest had a bit of congestion, and the doctor told me if I had put off treatment, I probably would have been very sick in a few days.

My neighbor had helped me focus on what was most important in that moment, and I was better off for her intervention.

It goes without saying that *God* is of utmost importance in my life 24/7. My faith underlies every breath I take. But given that foundation, I need to keep my earthly priorities properly aligned and at any moment focus on what is most important *now* in order to live the fulfilling, rewarding life I believe God wants his children to enjoy.

This morning, writing was a priority for me, but as the hours passed and health declined, something else became more important. Yet I was slow to acknowledge it until my friend called and made the obvious, well, obvious: I was sick and needed to go to the doctor to keep from getting sicker.

What is it that makes us put off doing something we know we need to do? For some reason, it often seems easier to think about other things rather than to focus on what's the most important thing *now*. Maybe that's because a most important thing can feel too needy and way too demanding in the present moment.

Focusing on what's important now means to live consciously. It means recognizing what's most important in this moment and not wanting to be anywhere else or do anything else with anybody else. I read once that when we "let go of wanting something else to happen in this moment, we take a profound step toward being able to encounter what is here now." Living consciously means we're simply mindful of focusing on this very moment in time, gratefully acknowledging the fact that we have it and are alive in it, and focusing on what is most important for *now*.

This morning I needed to drop the preconceived plan I had made—writing—and take care of the need at hand—my health. The whole thing boiled down to trusting God with and for this very moment and what was most important in it.

Being mindful of that relationship motivates us to face the important things in our lives with confidence, knowing God is in control. We may not understand what is happening or why, but we can have a trusting heart that God is in charge. And if we live from that center of focus, we will be consciously present every second of the day and mindful of what is important.

I'm reminded of the passage in Psalm 31:15 that says, "My times are in Your hand" (NKJV). As is so often the case, I'm asking the Lord to keep my eyes and heart open to whatever he wants me to do, moment by moment, trusting him to guide me in recognizing what is most important.

SIXTEEN

Decide What Is Not Necessary

After I moved into my current house in Texas, it took me three years to get around to cleaning out my closet, the big one that's just off the master bathroom with all my clothes in it. Crowded, unsightly, and embarrassingly messy, that closet lowered my spirit every time I went in there. Being a neatnik, I kept asking myself why I was waiting so long to clean it up. It finally hit me that I didn't do it because I didn't know what to keep and what not to keep. I couldn't figure out where to start. There were times I even thought about blasting that closet off the end of the house so I wouldn't have to look at it anymore.

One vulnerable day, fortified by a pot of coffee and empowering

Scriptures like "With God all things are possible" (Matthew 19:26 NKJV), I decided to take matters in hand.

I started by laying out three little governing rules.

First: clean the closet in geographical sections, first the NE corner, then the NW corner to the SE corner, so I wouldn't be overwhelmed right off the bat with the magnitude of the mess. Little by little, I followed that course. Working steadily but not hurriedly, I covered the entire closet in sections, and as I saw progress along the way, it strengthened my determination to keep going. Some days I'd spend a couple of hours and then stop until I had more energy; other days I'd work four or five hours. When I was sick of looking at piles of stuff, I just didn't go in there.

Second: any personal or family one-of-a-kind thing is an automatic keeper. This rule let me celebrate along the way when I found treasures that had been tucked away and forgotten. Oh, my gosh, the treasures! In two old cedar chests there were letters I had won in high school back in the forties for basketball, swimming, volleyball, and modern dance. I ran across ticket stubs from my performances with the Dallas Opera in the fifties and sixties, which brought back many wonderful memories. There were notes and letters in my father's handwriting from the seventies, written after my mother's death. I found old photographs from foreign trips I'd taken in the eighties, bunched together with original artwork from friends given to me at my retirement party in 1987. I tried on clothes (some of which I'd bought in the nineties), chose what I wanted to keep, and put the rest in bags to give away. (I won't even mention the old, full laundry bag I ran across that I'd misplaced about six months earlier—but, interestingly enough, not missed.)

Third: on the spot, determine what's necessary and not necessary to keep. By having this rule to go by, I didn't wind up with things I really didn't want, and I didn't put off making decisions I needed to make.

The unnecessary stuff was given to Goodwill, passed on to one of my brothers (if either of them wanted it), or tossed in the trash. In a few days, the closet was straight, clean, and organized. For months after that, when I went in my closet I'd do a 360-degree turn and stare. Seeing my orderly belongings pleased my heart and lifted my spirit.

I finally figured out the real reason I couldn't clean out that closet earlier: I was concentrating on what was *not* necessary, and I really didn't know what that was until I dug into all those stacks. Once I looked carefully at the things in my closet, the things I had loved and treasured through the years were easily separated from the items with no meaning.

We can decide what is *not* necessary to keep by simply making up our minds about what *is*. Nothing in life is more important than knowing what is essential, unless it's knowing what isn't.

{ SEVENTEEN }

Write Down the Important Things

When I think back on my childhood, I don't remember anybody ever telling me to "write that down." Nevertheless, something in me always wanted to take notes. To this day, I go around with a pen in my pocket or a pencil in my hand so I can write down appointments, commitments, lists, whatever. You may prefer to make note of the important things in your life on your smartphone, computer, iPad, or I don't know what else!

I write down lists of books I want to read, music I want to hear, movies I intend to see. The truth is, I often write down not only what I plan to do but also what I'm actually doing . . . or what I did. My pals may think it's weird (except when they call me because they've forgotten some detail of their own lives they're hoping I've jotted down somewhere).

I come from a long line of letter writers, note takers, jotters, journal keepers, authors, and poets. My grandmother used to write poems on the back of used envelopes, and I never got a post-card from her that didn't have a message in its proper spot as well as all around the edges in a circle where the words got smaller and smaller as they neared the end of her greeting. I still have a note Grandmother wrote to her children when they were little that read, "Gone next door to borrow an egg." I love that note because it was my grandmother to a T. Letting her family know where she was, and for what reason, was important to her—even to the point of leaving them a note that she's out of the house borrowing an egg.

I'm one who writes dates on almost everything I own. When I finish reading a book, I print the date of completion and sign my name on the last page. When I pay a bill, I stamp the invoice PAID, date it, and write the check number on it with my initials at the bottom. I've done it for years. I have a collection of jour-nals that cover the past twenty-five years, literally crammed with words describing my whereabouts, feelings, concerns, names, addresses, maps, directions, finances, and drawings. All this is important to me. That's why I write it down. It's second nature.

One of the primary reasons to write something down is because we're apt to forget it. And the older we get, the more apt we become. If I tell somebody I'll call him or her and then can't remember his or her phone number, it bothers me; so I write it down. When I go to the grocery store and forget why I went, that bothers me; so I write down a grocery list. If I promise somebody dinner at my house on a particular night and later have no idea when that night is because I didn't make a note of it, that bothers me; so I write it down. You get the picture. I write down what I might forget, which could be just about everything.

I've also written down my basic beliefs: I call it a credo. It's the twelve most important things in my life, out of which flows my value system. Anything that defines me is important for me to know, and I love seeing it in print. Every five or six years I read it again . . . just to see if my life is still making sense to me. It's similar to the mission statements many businesses, churches, and families draw up so that everyone in that group knows and understands the values that guide their activities and purpose.

And what about goals? I firmly believe I was able to take early retirement from business in great part because I wrote down that goal three years before it ever came to fruition. And personal goals? Financial? Travel? Physical? Each of these is very important when it comes to growth. With my goals written down, I have something to aim toward. They help me organize my time, thoughts, schedule, belongings—my life.

The most important thing for me to remember is the nature and nurture of God. I don't know where I'd be had I not written down notes from various Bible teachers through the years. Those notes have saved my life. They've not only instructed me but also comforted me and led me through heartaches. It's through studying the Word of God that I learned to believe, trust, forgive, endure, accomplish, and enjoy my relationship with him. Those notes directed me to the proper Scriptures I needed at different times in my life, and they continue to do so.

I hope when I die, I'll have a pen and paper in my hand and my friends will bury me with them. Sometimes we want to do something, but it's too hard, too expensive, too time consuming. But writing it down is none of the above. It's easy. You should try it.

{ EIGHTEEN }

Allow Yourself to Be Sad

Although I was never an avid fan of the Beatles, there are a few of their songs I really love. One of them is "Let It Be." They named an album with that title to make a statement about leaving problems behind and moving on in life. Paul McCartney wrote the song about his mother, Mary, who died when he was fourteen. He dreamed she came to him at a time when he was sad and in trouble, "speaking words of wisdom." Because her words comforted him and brought him peace, he wrote this song, which also includes the lyrics, "There will be an answer. Let it be."

McCartney's beautiful lyrics were, in part, a way to express the sadness in his heart. Growing up in a family that strongly encouraged being happy all the time, I had to learn how to express sadness without trying to hide it. I didn't know it was all right to let my sadness show. When I became an adult, I told a dear friend about how troublesome that dichotomy was, and she encouraged me to "lean into" my sadness—to feel it completely, not try to make it into some sort of fake happiness.

As time went on, I learned the value of feeling the entire range of my emotions. And it was only then that I understood I was really alive because I was able to feel my feelings—all of them. Interestingly, I also learned that some of my finest moments occur when I'm feeling unhappy, unfulfilled, uncomfortable—because through these moments I'm more likely to get out of my rut and look for other ways to answer life's hardest questions, as well as let my creative nature express itself.

I learned every zenith has a nadir, every high has a low. To know how fully we are living life, we need a basis of comparison as a standard. For example, we can't really know how well we are unless we've experienced true sickness. Nor can we know genuine victory until we've known defeat. By the same token, how can we know happiness in its fullness unless we allow ourselves to feel sad? It's by this basis of comparison we're able to equate the fullness we feel with the emptiness at the other end of the spectrum. If we build a wall around us to keep out sadness, we'll inadvertently keep happiness out, too. Therefore, we must allow ourselves to feel both.

Let me encourage you, when sadness comes, to "let it be." As it finds a place in your heart and moves through your spirit, it awakens creative genes that are waiting to find expression. Who knows? You may become another Franz Schubert or Vincent van Gogh. Their best compositions were born of their deepest grief— but look at the joy they brought to the rest of the world.

{ NINETEEN }

Acknowledge Your Need for Help

Leaving the dentist's office several years ago, I heard someone call out in a faint cry, "Help. Help. Can you help me?" I looked around the parking lot but saw no one. Then the cry came again. "Help me. Please help me."

I hurriedly followed the sound, and there on the asphalt lay an elderly woman with her head resting against the tire of a van. She had apparently missed her step coming off a curb into the lot and had fallen; now she was unable to get up.

Kneeling down quickly so she could see and hear me, I gave her my name and told her to lie still while I called for help. She had hit her forehead, which was bleeding a bit, and she had scratches on both her elbow and knee. I felt so bad for her. She told me her name was Martha, and she was trying to get to her car when she fell.

Within a few minutes, an ambulance arrived. As Martha was being loaded into the ambulance, I assured her I'd follow in my car and see her very soon at the hospital, which was just up the street.

I didn't know what to do, but I knew I wanted to be available for this woman if I could help her further. My heart went out to her. Even though she was a total stranger, it was obvious she needed help, and except for the ambulance personnel, I was the only one at the moment who knew that.

Shortly after Martha had been admitted, examined, and assigned a room, I went to her bedside and asked how she felt. Without hesitation, she said to me, "Oh, Luci, thank you so much for coming with me. I'm so clumsy, and I fall easily. Please promise me you'll stay with me and won't tell my daughter I fell. Will you promise me that?"

I admit I was a little shocked she didn't want her daughter to know of her fall. If she had been my mother, I certainly would have wanted to know—and I told her so. Once again, she insisted I not tell her.

"I think my daughter's tired of my asking for help," she said. "I'm too old for her to handle; I think she gets sick and tired of my asking her to do things for me."

As the day wore on and turned into evening and then nightfall, Martha and I talked more and more about her accident and the need to tell her daughter. I finally convinced her it was important for her family to know where she was and that she was all right. I knew they'd be worried. About 8:00 p.m., the daughter came; I met her and she was as kind as could be. She was genuinely grateful I had called her to let her know about her mother's need. Of course she wanted to know.

Martha had suffered a broken collarbone and was in the hospital a week. I visited her a couple of times and was so glad I had been able to be of assistance to her. I've thought about her many times through the years, and it's become a reminder to me of how difficult it can be to ask for help or even let someone come to our aid, including our own loved ones. I'm amazed at how self-sufficient we think we are.

Psalm 3:8 says, "Real help comes from God," and more often than not, he uses a person to provide that help. We're not created to be self-sustaining, self-sufficient, or self-centered. We need each other. In several different verses, the Bible talks about our being the "body of Christ," with each part, each one of us, having his or her own place and purpose.

Acknowledging our need for family, friends, or a caregiver is vitally important when it comes to our health and well-being. You may start thinking they don't care, or, like Martha, you may fear you're a burden on them. Don't assume that. With everything, there are appropriate boundaries. But I can tell you from experience, it's much more of a burden for your loved ones *not* to know when you need them.

One of the great lessons in life is finding the right balance between giving and receiving help from our loved ones. Or from total strangers. Ask Martha.

{ TWENTY }

Find Contentment in Doing Without

I once read a definition of contentment that stuck with me, probably because it reminds me that contentment has nothing to do with money, yet the people who live this way are millionaires in their souls. It's truly one of the primary secrets to a happy life:

> Keep your heart free from hate, your mind from worry, live simply, expect little, give much, sing often, pray always, forget self, think of others and their feelings, fill your heart with love, and scatter laughter wherever you go. These are the links in the golden chain of contentment.

I don't know the source of the definition, but I liked it so much I jotted it down in my journal years ago, and I've never forgotten it. Learning to do without is almost an art form because it's the opposite of *more*, which is what most of us want—or think we want. The best way to be content is to count our blessings, not our cash.

In the early days of 1993, I was faced with a lot of financial challenges and knew it was going to be a hard year for me regarding money. I made a list of things to consider before I spent a penny. There were twelve considerations on the list, and the twelfth was, "Do without."

I stuck that list in the front of my '93 journal and asked the Lord to help me remember those twelve items and not gripe about anything having to do with money, spending, saving, tithing, and investing. And, just for fun, next to the list I stuck a note I had received from a friend. It said, "The more you complain, the longer God lets you live." I knew that joke would help me keep my mouth shut when I wanted to gripe about having no money.

What a year that turned out to be:

- Instead of going to movies, I wrote poetry and read books.
- Instead of eating out, I cooked meals at home and made up recipes.
- Instead of buying birthday gifts or greeting cards, I made them myself.
- Instead of buying fresh flowers, I resurrected discarded mums out of Dumpsters—seriously!
- Instead of buying new music CDs, I listened again and again to the ones I already owned.
- Instead of calling my friends long distance, I wrote them long letters.

- Instead of tossing or giving away what was broken, I repaired it myself.
- Instead of fretting over what I couldn't do, I rejoiced over what I could.

That same year I got a whopping federal income tax bill I was totally unable to pay, but instead of worrying about it, I asked the Lord to guide my thoughts and steps so I'd know what to do. I took back some stuff I had purchased and got refunds, and I completely stopped buying anything I didn't absolutely need.

As hard as it is to believe, it all turned out to be kind of fun! I tightened my belt every way I could and took money out of a few investments and paid the IRS. The Lord brought me through it and taught me some very important lessons about handling money and about trusting him. I knew he was with me every step of the way.

Here's what happens when we count our blessings instead of cash: we confront the issues of everyday living and examine our inner feelings. In so doing, we find new responses that better satisfy our needs and the needs of the people closest to us.

{ PART THREE }

Achieving Balance

TWENTY-ONE

Build Yourself
a Small Library

It occurred to me the other day that being reared in a home that had books and treasured them set me on a path that has had many wonderful rewards. One of them is that my two brothers love books as much as I. Just last month I mailed both of them a copy of the book I was reading so we could share its contents. This is second nature to the three of us, and it all started with a small, insignificant collection of books in our childhood.

Yet it was my friend Kurt, who lived down the street from me back in the 1960s, who first encouraged me to create something I could call a *library*. We became friends as I discovered that Kurt liked to read; I liked to read too. He loved books; I loved books. He had a little library; I didn't.

One Saturday morning when he was at my house we started talking about our mutual love of books. He said, "You know, Luci, you could build a library right here in your living room if you wanted to. You have lots of books. Let's figure out how to do it. Okay?"

My bookshelves were bricks and boards, but they served the purpose well. Together, Kurt and I started classifying books and had the time of our lives. Since book cataloging is more of an art form than a science, we were in heaven.

We organized everything according to topic: art, biography, gardening, history, music, novels, poetry, theology, travel, and so on. I printed out small labels, and Kurt stuck them on the shelves under each appropriate section. In a matter of minutes, I knew where everything was, and in short order, I had the beginnings of what would in time become the most beautiful room in my home.

Eventually, we had everything categorized so that my gathering of books looked like a very professional collection that made me nearly swoon every time I walked through the living room. That happened in 1965, and to this day, I'm still building a library. My two brothers have personal libraries in their homes too. We agree with Mark Twain, who reportedly said, "The man who does not read good books has no advantage over the man who cannot read them."

My books are my friends. Some I know like the back of my hand; they've been with me through trials, and I've read them three, four, and five times. Others are new friends with whom I'm just getting acquainted.

Since I was a senior in college, I've been a member of book clubs. I vividly remember the first "big" book I bought. It was *The Columbia Historical Portrait of New York*, printed by Doubleday & Co.

in 1953; it's a large hardback that cost me about $25—a fortune when I bought it back in 1955. But from that moment on, I couldn't get my fill of books. Many times I bought small, inexpensive volumes published by Modern Library, one of which is *Out of Africa* by Isak Dinesen. I bought it in 1970, and it's one of my closest friends, even now—magnificent writing and an incredible story. I've read it three times. (And if you've not read it, you should plan on starting it as soon as you finish *this* book.)

Unfortunately, people often think that to have a home library, you have to be an upper-class citizen with first edition antique books and lots of money. Let me clear that up right now. Granted, I do have some beautiful, leather-bound books and a few antiques, but I also have hundreds of paperbacks, as well as beat-up, old, and torn copies of books that I treasure as much (if not more) than those with beautiful leather bindings for which I paid a pretty penny. Finding a good book that's a bargain to boot is just icing on the cake. Those are the ones you find at Goodwill and Salvation Army thrift stores, yard sales, friends-of-the-library shops, and all sorts of other places where recycled items are sold.

I'll be eighty years old when this book is published, and there's nothing in my home I treasure more than the 450-square-foot library I designed when my house was built in 2004. The library might have started small, but now it's a treasure trove of books I've collected for sixty years on every topic you can imagine. Not only do I have the first book I ever bought but also the book I bought yesterday, and every one in between.

{ **TWENTY-TWO** }

Establish Integrity in Your Life

When I was in the eighth grade, I was dashing out the door one morning so I could walk to school with my friends, when I remembered I needed notebook paper. I asked my mother for money to buy some after school.

That afternoon I stopped in the grocery store and bought the paper, and on the way out I spotted a package of macaroons and decided to get them too. I only had enough money for the paper, so I paid the cashier and stole the macaroons to eat on the way home. I was certainly not in the habit of stealing anything, but who was going to miss one little package of cookies?

Walking through a big field to get to my house, I ate the stolen macaroons as fast as possible, throwing away the packaging so there would be no evidence of my theft. By the time I got in the front door of the house, I was sick at my stomach from gorging—and from stealing.

My mother was peeling potatoes at the kitchen sink for dinner. Feeling exceedingly guilty, I went straight up to her and in one long run-on sentence said, "Mother-I-bought-the-notebook-paper-and-paid-the-man-and-on-the-way-out-the-door-I-stole-a-package-of-macaroons-and-ate-them-all-the-way-home-and-I'm-sick-at-my-stomach-and-I-think-I'm-gonna-die."

Long pause.

Mother put the knife down (a good sign), turned to me, and said very softly, "I beg your pardon?"

Oh, gosh. I've gotta repeat it? Once again I told her my dilemma.

Very calmly, she said, "Well, honey, you'll need to get your money because we're going back to that store now so you can pay the man for what you stole."

While she'd been willing to give me money for school supplies, I would be paying the restitution out of my own savings tucked away in my bedroom. I begged Mother not to make me go back to the store, but she wouldn't take no for an answer. She laid her apron aside, picked up the car keys, and said with all the self-restraint in the world, "Get your money and meet me in the car."

I was mortified. The last thing I wanted to do was find that guy and tell him I had ripped off a package of macaroons. But before long, we were backing out of the driveway.

On the way, I begged and pleaded with Mother to *please* not make me confess. "That guy thinks I'm a Christian, Mother. Don't make me go back in there and pay him for those cookies. I'm begging you," I said.

She kept her cool, driving on without saying a word. When we pulled up in front, she finally spoke: "Go in there. Find the man; introduce yourself and tell him what you've done. Then pay him for the cookies. I'll wait for you in the doorway."

Reluctantly, I walked in and looked for the manager. When I told him who I was and that I had stolen a package of macaroons, he did the strangest thing. He took the money for the cookies, looked straight into my eyes, and said, "Wow. We have a lot of kids who come in here and steal things, Lucille, but I've never ever had anyone come back and pay for what they stole. You must be a Christian."

When we got in the car, Mother thanked me for doing the right thing. "Now, let's go home and have dinner," she said. "You're probably hungry." Not once did she mention that episode again, and for many years, neither did I.

That incident made an indelible impression on me. I will never forget that day or the lesson I learned about being a person of integrity. I might not have known I needed to learn it, but my mother did, and she taught it to me by quietly standing her ground in doing what was right.

Integrity is demonstrated by how we behave when no one is looking. It starts inside us and grows into a lifelong collection of sound decisions based on discernment, good judgment, knowledge, and wisdom. As Shakespeare wrote, "This above all, to thine own self be true. And it must follow as the night the day, thou canst not then be false to any man."

{ TWENTY-THREE }

Engage People in Fun Conversation

One of the most enjoyable conversations I've ever had happened thirty-seven years ago when I was talking with a friend's daughter. Beth was eight at the time and as bright as a silver dollar: funny, astute, sweet, and exceedingly clever for a little girl her age. I loved our visit so much, I wrote about it in my journal.

When I asked Beth how she was doing, she told me she'd been chatting with Gertrude Sweatstein. Not knowing Gertrude, I inquired further.

"Oh, Luci, Gertrude is weird. She sleeps all day and night; she has ten children and is divorced. Her ex-husband is Dr. Bloodworth. He's a psy-chi-a-trist [pronounced with very deliberate speech] who found a lot of significance while picking through people's scalps."

I laughed heartily and stopped her right there. "Wait a second, honey. Who *are* these people? How did you meet them?"

Within the next few minutes Beth introduced me to a fascinating collection of characters who lived in her head. There was Mabel Chatican, a woman who cried all the time, talked through her tears, and had all the quirks of a strange bird right out of Charles Dickens. Two of the others were Mrs. Weatherworth, overwhelmed with life, and Colonel Stridesbaker, a tough army woman with a strong Texas accent.

After that initial conversation, Beth and I chatted many times about these people she had dreamed up. I loved them and loved talking with Beth about them because she could describe them perfectly.

As time went on, Beth and I left that group behind and enjoyed even more interesting visits. While chatting a couple of years later, Beth asked if she and I could have a philosophical conversation. "My mom told me she loves talking to you because the two of you have philosophical conversations. Can we have a conversation like that, Luci?"

"Of course."

Then she said, "What *is* a philosophical conversation? How do we do it?"

"Well, let's see . . ." I had to think for a few seconds. "It often starts with a *why* or *which* question."

"Like what?"

I thought for a minute and recalled that Beth had once told me she wished her piano teacher were a Christian. I asked if she remembered saying that. She did.

"Okay then, here's a philosophical question about that: *Why* do you wish she were a Christian?"

Beth looked at me lovingly and slowly said, "Maybe we shouldn't have a philosophical conversation." We both laughed heartily.

So many years have passed since those wonderfully fun verbal exchanges with little Beth; we've had a million philosophical conversations since then. She's in her midforties now with a master's degree in sociology and is married with children of her own. We can (and often do) talk about every subject under the sun, and it's just as fun and exciting today as it was in the early days of our friendship. Why? Because the root of fun conversation is *in* Beth.

If you want to have a blast conversing with friends, here are some suggestions for how to do it. They may sound simple, but I promise you, they're effective:

- Be warm and friendly to those around you.
- Listen carefully to what's being said.
- Ask fun, open questions.
- Smile when you talk.
- Think of interesting topics to discuss.

A few Sundays ago after church, a group of us had lunch with my brother Chuck Swindoll and his wife. In the course of visiting, I asked Chuck, "Which was harder—being a student at Dallas Theological Seminary or being president there, thirty-two years later?"

That question opened an hour of fun and very, very interesting dialogue, not only with Chuck, but also with everybody at the table. There was rapt attention, processing, laughter, other questions, comments, and enjoyment for all of us.

No one person was doing all the talking; everybody was totally engaged. Not only was it unforgettable, it had all of us wondering when we could meet again for lunch. Fun conversation always makes us hungry for more.

{ TWENTY-FOUR }

Remember to Notice Things Today

I once heard Diane Sawyer say, "The most important thing in life is to pay attention."

I *love* that phrase! There's so much to see, experience, watch, and enjoy in life. But many times we miss it simply because we're not *present*. Our minds are a million miles away. We're simply not paying attention.

It's been said that troubles and weeds thrive on lack of attention, so if we've got either in our lives, we need to stop and do a bit of uprooting. One of the Old Testament prophets emphasized that point when he wrote, "Use your eyes, use your ears, pay careful attention to everything" (Ezekiel 44:5).

About a year ago a friend gave me a book called *How to Be an Explorer of the World*, with the subtitle *Portable Life Museum*. Since I'm a nut for museums anyway, the idea of having a portable one really turns my crank. There are pages in the book for taking notes, making lists, drawing pictures, storing collections, recording data, and documenting objects. I mean, what's not to like? Obviously, this book was tailor-made for *me*.

So I put it to the test. I had an appointment with a doctor to check my left eye, in which I had undergone cataract surgery a couple of weeks earlier. On my way to the post-op examination, I decided to make it a point to look for things I'd never seen. In other words, I wanted to notice *everything*. I was on the lookout for findings I could record in my new portable-museum book. I even asked the Lord to make me conscious of hidden, unusual, or different objects, not only for my own enjoyment, but to be consciously aware of life around me.

Since the eye exam called for my "bad eye" to be dilated, a friend asked if she could drive me to the appointment. Hot dog! "Great idea," I said, knowing that plan would allow me to use my "good eye" for noticing things. Off we went, she watching the road, and I watching the countryside.

I saw several things I'd never noticed before and recorded them. But the clincher and winner, hands down, happened when we got to the doctor's office, which is on the second floor and has windows all around. Across the street there's a railway stop, and between that building and the doctor's office are telephone poles and high wires.

Of course I had seen the railway stop before and had watched people walking around over there, but I had never noticed the poles or high wires between the buildings, even though I'd been going to that doctor's office for several years. As I was noticing things that day, I realized that not only were the poles and wires new to me, but hanging on one of the high wires was a pair of tennis shoes somebody had thrown up there after tying the laces together. There they were, swinging in the breeze.

I was thrilled to death. What a find!

I asked three or four people who worked there how long the tennis shoes had been blowing around up there, and not one person had even noticed them. Every employee I asked said something like, "Oh, my gosh. Would you look at that? Wonder how long those have been there?"

Not only did I write about that in my book, I also wrote a little note of helpful criticism to myself: "STOP, Luci! Take note more often."

How frequently do we go through the day without any awareness of what's in front of us? We don't mean to be oblivious to the world around us, and it's not that we don't care. We just don't pay attention.

I challenge you to keep your eyes peeled and your heart open to God's unique, colorful, and sometimes humorous surprises in your life. It'll make your day brighter and a whole lot more fun. Try it. You'll like it. Write it down.

And while you're at it, write this down too. It's good advice: "You made me so happy, God. I saw your work and I shouted for joy. How magnificent your work, God! How profound your thoughts! Dullards never notice what you do; fools never do get it" (Psalm 92:4–6).

TWENTY-FIVE

Disregard What Isn't Your Business

When I worked in California many years ago, an engineer came into the drafting room one day where six or eight of us were working at our tables. We all knew him and could tell something was wrong. The guy (let's call him Fred) was furious. Another engineer, younger than he and with less seniority, had been promoted to a leadership position, and Fred was livid. He took off his hard hat, threw it across the room, and started telling us what happened and how mad he was at management. (In short order, it was easy to see why he didn't get the promotion.)

Those of us at the drafting tables just looked at him with a blank stare, trying to figure out what he wanted, and then we went back to work. Nobody said a thing—it was none of our business—so he eventually stalked out, madder than a wet hen.

A little later, Fred was fired from his job, and for the rest of us, life went on as usual.

There are times when stuff happens that's none of our business. We might want to say something, but if we're wise, we know better. We keep our mouths shut, turn away, and disregard the fact that it ever happened.

Knowing when to pay full attention, my topic in the previous chapter, and when to pay *no* attention, the focus of this chapter, is a matter of discernment. And, dare I say, discernment is a gift of years. Discerning when to pay no attention may be the harder choice.

Being by nature averse to conflict, it's easy for me not to get involved in situations like the one described above. I don't like confrontation, and if people argue in my presence, I often get a stomachache. It's always my first choice not to get involved in issues that have nothing to do with me.

Each of us needs to maintain an imaginary line in our thinking that we won't cross when something isn't our business. If somebody is verbally fighting at the next table in a restaurant, for instance, keep out of it. It's none of your business, or mine. If furious Fred bounces into your office, wanting you to choose up sides and tell off the management, keep out of that too.

I love 1 Thessalonians 4:11, the little verse that says, "Stay calm; mind your own business; do your own job." That *so* works for me.

Let me hasten to acknowledge, however, that there are times we do need to get involved, whether or not we want to. Maybe the word *disregard* in this chapter's title should be *discern*, because discernment is perception that comes through one of the senses or the intellect, and that's what I'm really talking about here.

I was with a dear friend a number of years ago on a road trip, and the two of us stopped at a crowded outdoor short-order shack of a place for ice cream cones. While we were there, a busload of Cub Scouts also stopped, and the little boys were running around, having a good time, while the Scout leader, a woman, was getting their ice cream and calling each of them to come pick it up. Little Ronnie didn't come when he was called, which made the woman mad. When he finally arrived, she was so upset, she yelled, "You brat. You come when I call you. Do you hear me?"

She slapped him on the head and knocked him to the ground.

I just stared and nearly dropped my teeth. But my friend? She stood up tall and very firmly said to the woman, "You're the brat. And if you hit him again, you'll have to deal with me."

I'm telling you, I could have crawled under a rock, I was so embarrassed. While I was coming to my senses, every person in the area (except for the Scout leader and me) was applauding my friend. She was simply not going to put up with child abuse, and that day I learned that neither should I—no matter how humiliated or embarrassed I might have been.

We all have to decide for ourselves what is none of our business. We have to set our own limits. Some limits are very clear, and others involve weighing options, making judgments, discerning truth, drawing boundaries, and considering all that's involved. I can't answer for you—and you can't answer for me. But God can answer for both of us, and we can ask him to guide us.

{ TWENTY-SIX }

Think Before You Say It

Wisdom is a virtue. A wise person thinks before she speaks. Talking too much usually reflects thinking too little. Recently I found these fantastic verses in Ecclesiastes 5:2–3 and was surprised to see how the Bible states this advice so clearly: "Don't shoot off your mouth, or speak before you think. Don't be too quick to tell God what you think he wants to hear. God's in charge, not you—the less you speak, the better."

That passage leaves no room for doubt, does it? Have you ever noticed how impossible it is to retrieve your words once they fall out of your mouth? I've known a few people who need a rewind button close to their lips so they can surreptitiously roll back words, sentences, or paragraphs that should never have been uttered in the first place. One of them is a very dear friend to whom I am devoted for life. I love her company, admire her enormously, and would lay down my life for her, but there is one thing I would love to change about her, and she knows it. In her enthusiasm about almost everything, she often blurts out something she wishes she hadn't said—or I wish she hadn't. She simply doesn't stop to think before she speaks.

For example, it's not unusual for her to be so enthusiastic about a piece of good news I've told her privately that she eagerly blurts it out publicly because she wants to share it with the world. The second she remembers it wasn't hers to tell, she quickly apologizes to me and wants to punch her little rewind button—but there isn't one. Oops! Through the years the two of us have often laughed at this quirkiness in her because she absolutely means no harm; it's just that her enthusiasm gets the best of her.

Many years ago, when we hadn't known each other very long, the two of us planned a little weekend trip over a holiday that we had decided to celebrate together. In talking with an acquaintance of hers, my friend offhandedly said to her, "Hey, you can come with us if you want," never thinking her friend would accept. But she did.

Later, when she was confessing that there would be three of us instead of two on the trip, she said it had never occurred to her that she should have asked me first, even though the plans were initially for just the two of us. So the three of us went on the trip, which was fine; but when I think back on it, the incident seems like an example of enthusiasm run amok, if there is such a thing.

Proverbs 27:6 says the wounds inflicted by a friend are more precious than the flattery of an enemy. Since I believe this (and so does my friend), I've asked her many times through the years to please talk to me before she commits me to do something or go somewhere or before she represents me in any way. I've said, "Think before you say it."

She's been very teachable, and while she doesn't have what I would call a perfect record, she's doing much better these days. She always means well, but unfortunately her enthusiasm still occasionally causes regret—both in her and in others.

How many times have you or I reacted negatively or thoughtlessly to a friend (or even a total stranger) with words we wish we could retract? I've seen women say unkind things to their husbands in social settings and felt uncomfortable for how it must have made the husband feel. I've watched total strangers yell obnoxiously at store clerks and airport workers. I've witnessed kids being rude to their parents and parents harshly scolding their children. And it could all be different, if we just stopped and used our brains before we opened our mouths.

Jesus put it best: "It's your heart, not the dictionary, that gives meaning to your words. . . . Words are powerful; take them seriously" (Matthew 12:34).

{ TWENTY-SEVEN }

List Your Thoughts and Dreams

Did you know the first word Picasso ever said was *pencil*? I have a feeling it was my first word too. I've loved pencils all my life, and if pencil and paper are close at hand, I'm a happy girl. So it stands to reason that I love lists. I make them constantly: what I do, what I want to do, what I've done. Laugh if you will, but I believe making lists is one of the most important secrets to a happy life. And best of all, it's simple; it requires no money, no skill, no education, no schedule. No kidding! Just write it down, and there you go.

My proclivity for list making began when I was about the age of twelve and people started asking me what I wanted to be when I grew up. Believe it or not, I knew! I'd made a list—written down what I wanted for my life: I knew I wanted to go to college and work in an office. I wanted to sing on a stage and learn other languages. I wanted to travel all over the world and meet people from other countries. I wanted to read lots of books and maybe even write a book one day. I had no idea how I'd manage to do all I wanted to do, but that didn't matter. What mattered was that I had written it down on my to-do list.

God also has a to-do list for us. He creates us uniquely and has dreams and plans for our lives. As we take one baby step at a time, he opens doors and in his still, small voice whispers, "This is the way, walk in it" (Isaiah 30:21 NKJV). The joy of my entire life has come from my dependence on him as he has both fulfilled my desires and changed them. I've learned to trust God because I'm very intentional about and cognizant of his leadership.

Let me tell you what he did. In May 1959, there was a small article in the *Dallas Morning News* that reached out to me. The opening sentence read, "Dallas Civic Opera will hold chorus Auditions May 29 and 30 at Maple Theater for its 1959 season at State Fair Music Hall."

The piece went on to say what operas would be performed and on what dates. I'd learned an aria in college, so with that under my belt, I auditioned. And folks, the rest is history! I was accepted into the chorus and sang with the Dallas Opera for fifteen years, from 1959 through 1973, when I moved to Southern California.

What happened as a result of that audition proves the truth of Ephesians 3:20–21: "God can do anything, you know—far more than you could ever imagine or guess or request in your wildest dreams! He does it not by pushing us around but by working within us, his Spirit deeply and gently within us."

By my being an opera chorister, the door opened for me to work onstage with many interesting people, including opera stars Dame Joan Southerland, Placido Domingo, and Maria Callas.

Many wonderful things resulted from my desire to sing onstage that were never even on my to-do list. I took lessons in Italian and traveled abroad. I met people from other countries and visited in their homes. Through that one dream, God gave me much more than I could have asked for or even imagined. I doubt I would be doing what I am today, in fact, if my life had not taken the path it has.

Truthfully, we have no idea what God is going to do in and through the life he's given us. Scripture says he can do anything. *Anything.* Within the confines of our hearts, he is doing things this very minute about which we know nothing. He's opening doors, putting out fires, rearranging schedules, making crooked places straight. He's gently molding and making us into what he wants us to become while opening pathways to get us there, whispering, "This is the way; walk in it."

Making a list of thoughts and dreams has been an amazing experience for me. Not because God takes his cues from my to-do list but because it serves as the map I can look at to see how far he's brought me.

I strongly urge you to make a list of your heart's desires, no matter your age. Someday you can actually trace how those dreams deeply and gently came to fruition by God's Spirit.

{ TWENTY-EIGHT }

Rise to the Occasion Often

I read something interesting the other day about aging. For the first time in history the number of people under the age of seventeen and those over sixty-five will be almost equal by the year 2030. That means Americans are living well into old age.

Scientists say that while we older people may not be as sharp on the computer as those who are younger, we think as well as the young . . . but differently. (Good to know!) We in the older generation think with more reflection, depth, and awareness. We may not be as fast at processing data as our younger friends, but instead of manipulating it, we reduce it to concepts and live out of those concepts.

The reason this is valuable to know is that some of you who are reading this are as old as I am (seventy-nine) or older, but you may be thinking it's time to give up, drop out of life, and let somebody else be responsible for whatever challenges come down the pike. Yet, believe it or not, now is the time *we* need to be the sages of the world. We're the ones who must evaluate, intercede, bring experience to bear, and rise to the occasion when need be. By virtue of age, we're the mentors for those who follow in our footsteps. We need to do the things that need to be done.

My maternal grandmother was a perfect example of one who rose to the occasion often. I was a teenager when she was well into her sixties, and I grew up understanding she was sharp as a tack. She taught piano, sang in the church choir, entertained guests in her home right and left, made gifts for her friends, and was personally acquainted with practically everybody in her little Texas town. We kids called her Momo, although her real name was Jessie Lundy. My grandfather, Orville, was an insurance salesman, but when money was tight, Momo rose to the occasion and found ways to bring in income too. She sold boxes of greeting cards. And since she knew almost everybody in town, she made a killin', as we say in Texas. Some months we laughed because she brought in more revenue than Granddaddy.

Momo's greatest gift, though, was throwing parties. She thrived on getting folks together and finding ways for everybody to be entertained. If they were lonely or blue or feeling left out, they'd be invited to Momo's for dinner and an evening of laughter and fun. I well remember, as a young girl in the 1940s, our family going to Momo's home in El Campo for the weekend. On Saturday night she invited all her neighbors and church friends over for a party. My brothers and I performed in the living room: one brother playing piano, one quoting poetry, and I mimicking Danny Kaye in patter songs from his movies. We all laughed, sang, danced, and carried on, meeting new people and enjoying old friends. Momo was in her element, bringing joy to everybody she knew.

Even when my grandmother began showing her age and wasn't feeling her best, she managed to get on a bus, come visit us in our home in Houston, and encourage us to see the bright side of life. She used to say, "A day is wasted unless we fall over in a heap laughing." What a spirit she had for life. Not only was she loved, but needed. She helped us see the rainbow instead of the clouds. Her very presence gave us purpose in life. She loved the Lord with all her heart and showed it in a thousand ways. By stepping up to the plate as long as she lived, she delivered a home run every time.

My emphasis so far in this chapter has been on older folks who rise to the occasion, but all of us, no matter what age we are, need to be ready to do what needs to be done in whatever circumstances surround us. Think how inspiring it is to see teenagers stepping up to mow an elderly neighbor's lawn—or volunteering for mission trips to impoverished areas of the world. Consider what an impression a busy young mother makes when she steps in to help care for the children of a military spouse in her church or neighborhood so he or she can deal with an emergency—or just take a break—while the husband or wife is serving abroad. A friend told me how amazed she was one Christmastime to be hurrying into a discount store and realize the guy standing out in the cold alone, ringing the bell over the Salvation Army collection kettle, was a top administrator at the state university in that town. That bell needed to be rung, and volunteers were in short supply; sure, the college administrator was busy, but he saw the need, put on his coat, and stepped up to serve. We see people rise to the occasion often, and we're inspired to follow their example.

I believe it's our duty to rise to the occasion as often as possible.

Life is a spiritual responsibility, a moral force around us with challenging tests. It's not some private enterprise we live unto ourselves. As Christians, we have a calling to live Christlike lives even in tough times. The first chapter of James gives a clear picture of that calling: "Consider it a sheer gift, friends, when tests and challenges come at you from all sides. You know that under pressure, your faith-life is forced into the open and shows its true colors. . . . Anyone who meets a testing challenge head-on and manages to stick it out is mighty fortunate. For such persons loyally in love with God, the reward is life and more life" (vv. 2–3, 12).

TWENTY-NINE

Thank Others for Their Efforts

Isn't it interesting what the two words *thank you* can do? It's been said that gratitude is the most exquisite form of courtesy.

As I write this, it's Sunday afternoon, and this morning in church, the message was on the value of saying thank you to those around us who often go unnoticed or ignored.

There was a reference to people in uniform—military, postal service letter carriers, police officers, and firefighters—as well as to those who perform thankless jobs, such as garbage collectors and street sweepers. What about the person who checks you out at the grocery store or the woman on the phone who makes your flight reservations?

It might be easy to remember to thank family members or coworkers for gifts and favors: passing the mashed potatoes, giving us a ride home when our car's in the shop, surprising us with a birthday present. But what about the big-picture things our family members do for us?

I asked a friend who has a young son about seven years old, what is the hardest thing about motherhood? She thought for a minute, then gave me a wonderful answer: "Everything is critical." I loved that! I'm sure it's true. Wouldn't it be nice when her little boy grows up to say to his mother as a grown man, "Thank you for the years you did things for me. Not only did you pick up my clothes, do my laundry, help me with my homework, see that I got places on time, teach me how to be nice and get along on the playground, but you also got me where I am today because you knew *everything* mattered. I just want to thank you for that, Mom."

Most women would probably faint if their grown kids said that. Yet what a wonderful thing it would be.

When I was in high school, I played the cello. Primarily I'm a singer, but everybody in my family played an instrument, so I wanted to play one too. Just for fun and at bonfire parties, I played the ukulele, but when I was offered an opportunity to play cello in orchestra class, I said yes. I've always loved the sounds that come from the cello, but I had no idea how difficult it was to play. Nevertheless, I was determined to learn. Little by little I improved, but I never was what one would call good. However, my high school music teacher, Mr. Seastrand, who could play every instrument beautifully, encouraged me to keep at it. I was even given a little solo part in one of the pieces our orchestra played. I was scared to death I'd botch it, so I practiced hours on end to do it well. When the performance was over, Mr. Seastrand said to me, "Lucille, you played beautifully tonight. You really made that solo part *sing*. Every note was on pitch. Just think, one day you might be a famous cellist. You never know. Thank you for a job well done."

I couldn't wait to tell my parents and write that in my diary. It was one of the nicest, sincerest compliments I've ever gotten—and coming from him, it was unbelievable. You can tell it meant a lot because that was sixty-five years ago, and I've never forgotten it. Here's what really made that compliment stand out: Mr. Seastrand didn't just say the usual, "Good job," that so many of us toss off to performers we know or encounter. He said *thank you*, acknowledging the hard work I'd done to prepare for my solo.

A cellist played the offertory in church this morning just before the message on thankfulness. The two parts of the service made me think of Mr. Seastrand's words, which reminded me of the deep value of gratitude. It costs us nothing to thank someone else, but to the person receiving our thanks, our words may be priceless—and unforgettable.

{ THIRTY }

Acquire a Brand-New Skill

My friend Scott is paraplegic. When he was seventeen he was in a motocross accident, and his spinal cord was severed in two places. Hospitalized for twenty-eight days, Scott was told by one of his doctors he should get used to the fact he would no longer have a normal life. It was doubtful he'd ever have a job, a home, or a family of his own. In an effort to prepare Scott for the worst, the doctor told Scott to resign himself to being confined to a wheelchair the rest of his life—and all that meant.

In contrast, Scott's mother looked at his circumstances very differently. She told Scott that while it was true he would be in a wheelchair, the only thing he couldn't do was walk. Everything else was up to him, and with the right spirit he could do anything he wanted.

Tremendously motivated, he started dreaming about what he could do and stopped limiting himself by dwelling on what he couldn't.

Scott is now forty-three and happily married with a nine-year-old son, Garrett. Having giant-sized willpower, Scott does more than most men who are able-bodied. He is strong and physically fit. He drives a car, mows the grass, cleans the house, plays on a tennis team, and skis on both water and snow. He's built a barn and a fence on the acreage around his home. He delights in coaching Garrett's basketball team and riding four-wheelers with him. He takes his family camping and jet skiing.

Scott is a wonder. Truly, he can do everything but walk. And even now, he's learning new skills. Because of his innate verve and a mother who encouraged him to be courageous, he's learned how to do things that defied that doctor's grim prediction all those years ago.

Learning new skills can be challenging, but it can also lead us to the most enjoyable, rewarding activities in life. Yet some of us are very hesitant. We worry, *Am I good enough? Strong enough? Fit enough? Brave enough? Do I have enough money or training?* Or maybe, as adults, we learn new skills out of necessity and figure, why should we tackle any more than we have to?

If this is your attitude, here's a suggestion: learn something *fun*. Instead of sitting for hours in front of a TV or computer or electronic game killing time, consider learning how to . . .

- **Knit**: It can be fun—and rewarding—to learn how to create something from "nothing." I had a friend who became so good at this skill she knitted a pair of gloves while watching a movie.

- *Juggle*: Picture the day you throw three balls in the air and can actually keep them there.
- *Yo-yo*: I once met the world champion, who was so good he made the yo-yo land in his pocket.
- *Play the harmonica*: My harmonica-playing dad was in high demand at parties.
- *Sketch*: For me, time flies when I draw pictures of the people, places, or things around me.
- *Build something*: One of my former coworkers and his wife built a boat and lived on it.

When you're learning a fun new skill, you're not trying to impress somebody; you're just enjoying one of the secrets to a happy life. Your pursuit of a new interest or your learning of a new skill can even help you make new friends. And if none of these physical skills appeals to you, dream up your own. Set goals, start small, invite friends to join you, and have the time of your life.

But if you don't want to do something physical, how about working on a few mental skills? We all need improvement in those. Here's a list for starters, but feel free to make your own:

- Coping with life
- Staying calm
- Enjoying solitude
- Managing your time
- Laughing at yourself
- Practicing your faith

As long as we're alive, we have the ability to learn. When you hear a voice in your head whispering that you can't do something, think about Scott or others you know who have overcome challenges and learned a new skill.

Life's too short to wait until everything is perfect or until you can walk on water before acquiring a new skill. That day will never come. Start right here, right now. Start with what you have without worrying about what you don't.

{ PART FOUR }

Living a Good Life

{ THIRTY-ONE }

Get Doctrine Under Your Belt

The year I graduated from college, I moved home to Houston to live with my parents for a couple of years. During that time my mom and dad, younger brother, and I went to a sound, Bible-teaching church. (My older brother had married and was living elsewhere.) The Bible classes we attended were held four nights a week, and I can't remember ever missing a single one. I *lived* to go to that Bible class, and each week I took copious notes. I couldn't seem to absorb enough teaching about God, his Word, and his ways. I was a sponge that fell in the ocean and drank it dry. For example, even though I had read 2 Timothy 3:16–17 many times with my family, when we studied it in that class, I really understood, for the first time, what it meant: "Every part of Scripture is God-breathed and useful one way or another—showing us truth, exposing our rebellion, correcting our mistakes, training us to live God's way. Through the Word we are put together and shaped up for the tasks God has for us."

Doctrinal teaching instructed me how to live the Christian life. I learned doctrines that clarified the Bible and God the Father, Son, and Holy Spirit. I studied doctrines regarding humanity, sin, salvation, the church, and the end times that will come one day. A world of data and information was opened up to me and set me on a new path.

I learned the Ten Commandments were written under the law of God and—*most importantly*—I now live under the wonderful grace of God. And living under grace, I learned that the culture, my past, peers, fears, even my feelings could no longer dictate my way of life. I learned that walking by faith I could please God, know him, and enjoy a lifetime in his presence.

For a good part of my young life, my feelings had ruled my behavior. And when those feelings fluctuated, so did my actions. But once I got a solid foundation of doctrine under my belt, I understood that *no matter how I felt*, God still loved me and his Spirit would be with me—guiding, forgiving, leading, caring, encouraging me regardless of my feelings, because biblical doctrine doesn't fluctuate. It's as solid as a rock. Through faith, I trusted God and his Word.

To embrace doctrinal teaching and make it one's own, three factors are essential: accepting the fact that all Scripture is God-breathed, understanding the structure of how Scriptures are written, and having a clear interpretation of scriptural truths. Doctrine is a system of teachings that relate to a particular subject. In this case, when I talk about biblical Christian doctrine,

I mean revelations in the Bible about God and humanity. It's as simple as that—and as difficult as that.

As a young girl, I placed my faith in Jesus Christ and invited him into my heart, but back then the only thing I knew for sure about the Bible was the gospel: Christ died for my sins and rose from the dead, and by trusting him as my Savior, I was forgiven of my sins, had an eternal home in heaven when I died, was assured that God loved me completely and that I could do nothing to lose my salvation. By virtue of my redemption, I was to share this good news with everybody I met. I believed that, and I lived solely out of that belief.

While all those truths are absolutely wonderful, and certainly life changing, and although I'd been an active church member forever, I knew little or nothing about the deep truths that help a person *grow* in faith. My sweet parents and brothers didn't have that foundation, either, until we all began attending the wonderful Bible class that changed *everything*.

So, in my opinion, a working knowledge of biblical doctrine may just be the most important factor to having a happy life because it puts and keeps everything in one's life in proper perspective. *Selah*.

{ THIRTY-TWO }

Look for Ways to Help

It was a long time before I knew the Bible talked about something many call the "gift of helps." I was acquainted with more prominent spiritual gifts like evangelism, teaching, prophesying, healing, and so forth. But a *gift* of *helping others*? I hadn't a clue. The idea comes from 1 Corinthians 12:27–28, which makes reference to those of us in the universal church having various parts to play. Those parts are defined by one's spiritual gifts being used to keep things going.

In retrospect, I can tell you for sure my mother had the gift of helps. She seemed to sense the needs of others and meet those needs without effort. It was second nature for her to take food to neighbors who were sick or recovering from surgery, bring groceries to folks who had no car, invite people to join us when they were alone. I loved that trait in her. I love it in anyone.

The spiritual gift of helping others is generally manifested in a servant attitude. Being responsive to the needs of others, the helper does whatever it takes to get the task accomplished. Interestingly, the Greek word in Scripture for *helps* means "to take instead of." It's doing the work of another. A beautiful word picture!

I have two friends who share a home together in my neighborhood, and they both have this wonderful spiritual gift of helps. They're forever looking for opportunities to be of assistance. It's not that they actually have *time* to help; they just *think* to help. It's a gift. More often than not, when either of them goes to the mall, the discount store, the grocery market, the cleaners, or anywhere else, they ask if they can run an errand for me while they're out. And even if I say no thank you, they will very likely show up on my doorstep later with a little surprise. A love gift!

When the home in which I now live was being built, one of them (who had overseen the work of building her own home nearby) worked every day with my builder whenever I was away on trips or speaking engagements, just to be sure things were done to my liking. And the minute I moved in, the other one volunteered to help me set up shop—putting books on shelves, arranging my kitchen, hanging clothes, unpacking boxes. As she engaged others to join in, it all became more like a party than a chore. My friend's attention to every detail never stopped. While she and her housemate are very different in terms of their gifts, they both serve and help friends all over the neighborhood. I'm beginning to think the gift of helping might be contagious!

Last spring their washing machine broke right in the middle of a huge load of laundry and water went *everywhere*. When they called to ask if they could bring their wet clothes to my house to wash them, I was thrilled to death. While one contacted a plumber, the other walked into my garage dragging behind her a huge black trash bag crammed with wet clothes. Together we hoisted it up into the utility sink and put the clothes in the washing machine. She was so apologetic I could hardly get out my words of gratitude. As I was waxing eloquent about how thrilled I was to help them with this problem, my friend smiled and said, "Luci, this isn't all. I've got six more bags full of wet towels in the trunk of my car. We used every towel in the house to mop up water. May I leave you those to wash?" I can't even tell you what it meant to me to be able to say, "Oh, my gosh! Yes!" to these friends who had done so much for me. And I meant every word of it. I washed, dried, and folded clothes and towels for the next six hours, listening to music as the work got done. I loved helping with this unexpected problem.

Trust me, you don't have to have the "gift of helps" to say to a friend, "May I do that for you?" Even if it's a person you have never seen before in your life, when you extend a helping hand it creates joy in both you and the recipient of your help. There's something about finding happiness in helping others that's indescribable.

I love serving those who need a lift. Maybe it's verbal encouragement. Maybe it's a ride when their car breaks down. Maybe it's a letter, an e-mail, or a visit because they're lonely. Maybe it's a meal together—and picking up the tab. Maybe it's just doing the laundry for friends whose washer breaks down. God gives us opportunities for all these things, and much more, when we simply reach out with a helping hand.

Second Corinthians 1:6–7 says it quite well: "If we are treated well, given a helping hand and encouraging word, that also works to your benefit, spurring you on, face forward, unflinching. Your hard times are also our hard times. When we see that you're just as willing to endure the hard times as to enjoy the good times, we know you're going to make it, no doubt about it."

{ THIRTY-THREE }

Tell It Like It Is

In 1989 I wrote a book called *Quite Honestly: A Journal of Thoughts and Activities for Daily Living*. My friend Carla helped me create the artwork, and together we provided the reader an opportunity to say what he or she honestly felt during fifty-two weeks in any given year. It was a place for the reader to "tell it like it is" day after day. Being one who loves journaling, I wanted to encourage people to be open, honest, real, and unafraid.

I've kept journals many years of my life and have recorded my thoughts and activities. Of the forty-six journals I've filled, there's not one that isn't precious to me. And when asked the question, "If your house were on fire, what would you grab first?" I can answer without hesitation, "My journals." That would be an armload, I know, but it's the truth. These journals chronicle my life. They contain my joys, sorrows, changes, fears, goals, dreams, desires, regrets, concerns, and imaginations.

When he was about my age, E. B. White wrote, "Even now, this late in the day, a blank sheet of paper holds the greatest excitement there is for me—more promising than a silver cloud, and prettier than a red wagon." I totally agree.

Look at a few ways journaling helps us enjoy happy lives:

- *Knowing ourselves.* When we take time to write in a journal, we open our hearts honestly but privately. We cry, laugh, fret, worry, cheer, feel, and process everything as deeply as we like without anyone criticizing or caring—or knowing. Being autobiographical is an excellent medium for revealing the truth about ourselves.
- *Gathering facts.* Think of the people whose legacy is found in their journals: Eugene Delacroix, Leo Tolstoy, Queen Victoria, and Anne Frank, to name a few. Because of gathered facts that were written in their diaries and journals, stories were saved that would have otherwise been lost.
- *Enjoying solitude.* While alone, we might feel lonely or aimless. But having a journal gives us the feeling there's a friend in the room who knows and accepts us. Telling the journal how things are going is like talking with a loved one.
- *Referencing memories.* When we can't remember dates, facts, and resolutions, it's quite likely they're somewhere in our journals. With a little time, we can go back through them and find what we're racking our brains to remember.
- *Feeling nostalgic.* Oh, the times I've reread entries about parties, reunions, and journeys with family members

or friends who are dear to me. There they are in my handwriting for me to rediscover in the stories that took place many years ago.

- *Asking questions*. The best conversationalists I know are those who ask good questions, and a journal is a perfect place to ask them of yourself first. This creates an environment to figure out what you want to say and how to word it.

- *Writing books*. For an author, journals are invaluable; they keep facts available forever. You can't imagine how often I've looked up activities that happened way back when, just to get my information straight. And it's right there in front of me, accurate, because I wrote it down when it happened.

When we see or feel something, more often than not we want to verbalize it. How frequently have we said, "I need to write that down so I won't forget it"? A journal is the place to do it. By telling how our life was lived, we leave a trace of who we really are. Or were.

I love Oscar Wilde's statement about his own journal, and I feel the same way about mine. "I never travel without my diary," he said. "One should always have something sensational to read in the train."

THIRTY-FOUR

Know for Sure
You're Insured

I was hospitalized in 2003 for a troublesome condition called atrial fibrillation. It was first thought to be a heart attack, but after a few days of medical care and attention, the doctors determined my heart was simply out of sinus rhythm. It righted itself on the third day, and I was dismissed. All of that was an interesting episode to me, but the most astounding thing happened when I got the bill. It was $33,000! Also amazing was the amount I actually owed on that invoice: $420. That's it! I still have the canceled check to remind myself of the importance of having health insurance.

Ironically, about that same time a dear friend who had no health insurance was hospitalized for surgery. She is a few years younger than I and didn't believe in having health insurance. Much later she told me when her costs were added up and sent to her, she owed somewhere between $75,000 and $100,000. She looked me straight in the face and said, "Luci, what was I thinking when I decided not to get health insurance? I must've been crazy. I had to take out a huge loan to pay that bill, and now I'm struggling to pay it off. I have the feeling I won't ever get out of debt."

A young girl from Oxford, Ohio, died in 2009 a few days shy of her twenty-third birthday. At an urgent care unit she was diagnosed with swine flu and pneumonia, but her condition got worse when she refused to go to the hospital for proper treatment because she had no health insurance. Of course, she might have died anyway, whether or not she had gone to the hospital. My point is that she felt she had no choice simply because she wasn't insured.

I recently read an alarming statistic that said 30 percent of nineteen- to twenty-four-year-olds refuse to get health insurance so they can have more spending money. Sadly, there are many older adults who apparently feel the same.

As you can see, I'm a firm believer in having insurance. My father was an insurance salesman when I was young, and our family was "insurance poor," as they say. I have no idea how much Daddy spent annually on insurance, but he was very conscientious about insuring everything he could: life, health, automobile, and home. Even though the policies were rarely used, they were in place if needed. My dad was a living example of what Suze Orman teaches: "Hope for the best, prepare for the worst."

There are lots of reasons why people need to be insured, but the main reason is protection. And part of being protected is knowing what your policy says. Again, I follow my father's example and do as he did. I'm aware of what my policy covers in the event of a problem. I suppose there's a lot of jargon that people don't read, or don't understand when they do. Nonetheless, it's important to spend time figuring out what you have.

I want to say this with all the love in the world, but very seriously: if you don't have insurance, get it. To those of you who say you trust the Lord to take care of you, I would also say very seriously: God gave you a brain. Use it! Until we move on to heaven, we live in an imperfect world where bad things happen. Insuring the resources and gifts God has given you in this life is good stewardship.

Even if you have to cut out something else, don't try to live without insurance. I consider it mandatory to having a happy life. I can tell you from experience, overwhelming debt that rules your life will eat you up alive. My friend is living proof that debt can result when one isn't properly insured. Part of being happy is knowing how to manage money, and some of that money must go into insurance policies, otherwise you'll spend it paying off the debt you incurred because you didn't think you needed it. It's as simple as that. I ain't eighty for nuthin'!

{ THIRTY-FIVE }

Batten Down All the Hatches

Much of my childhood was spent at Carancahua Bay, a small inlet along the southern coast of Texas, not far from Palacios. My grandfather owned a cabin there, where our family went on vacation. It was a place where we could swim, fish, sleep outdoors, meet relatives for family reunions, and have a high ole time inexpensively. We loved it.

My dad's favorite pastime was fishing, so to him these vacations were sheer bliss. The only one in the family who didn't give a hoot about fishing was my older brother, Orville. Nevertheless, because we were too young to be left in the cabin by ourselves, Orv had to go with us. Instead of fishing, he'd sit on the bow of the boat working miracles with his chemistry set while the rest of us caught the evening's meal. I always had a fear he'd blow our ship out of the water, but thank goodness we were spared.

Often while fishing we saw clouds gathering on the distant horizon, indicating a storm was coming. Drops of rain would begin to fall and the wind would pick up. If we ignored those signs and stayed out too long, a waterspout whirlwind might form in the shape of a tornado. Then a progressive gyrating mass of air would erupt into a violent and sudden downpour. I remember these occasions well, because my dad's instruction was always the same, "Batten down the hatches—now!"

Oh, brother! That's all it took: we hurriedly pulled in our fishing lines, tied the "catch bucket" to one of the seats, threw the rest of the bait overboard, and held on to our hats while Daddy started the motor and took off for safety. We'd go top speed back to the boathouse. I can still hear Orv saying, "Daddy, don't go so fast! My beaker's gonna blow away."

But Daddy wouldn't slow down. Danger was lurking, and he felt responsible to get us out of it. We all held on tightly and zoomed to the shoreline.

"Batten down the hatches" is a nautical term meaning to close the doors or openings on a boat before a storm hits. It's become an American idiom meaning to prepare and protect yourself in every way possible for whatever life storm is coming. Since my preteen years, I've used that phrase to remind myself to start getting ready for trouble whenever I sense it lurking on the horizon. And that trouble can come in different forms: anxiety, fear, poor health, aging, lack of money, and letting go of something, to name a few.

We don't have to be rocket scientists to know we should prepare for what *might* happen when these circumstances occur. For example, we might have to make a difficult decision that will determine the quality of life for our remaining years. We might have to forfeit well-laid plans. We might need to forgive an enemy. We might have to look into asking, or even hiring, others to help us instead of tackling our problems alone. Whatever it is, we must consciously decide what is best for ourselves and then *do* it. Battening down all the hatches is *not* a time to do nothing.

By sharing this step to a happy life, I'm encouraging all of us to confront the storms of life with acceptance, fortitude, and grace. Scripture provides a perfect guideline for the best way to face these problems. It's found in Mark 14:38, which says, "Stay alert, be in prayer, so you don't enter the danger zone without even knowing it. Don't be naive."

When we know danger is up ahead, preparation, prayer, and patience will get us through.

The last time I was with my father in a boat, a squall came up that scared me. As a young teenager, I kept thinking we'd never make it to shore because the waves were so high and strong. While Daddy was busy working the motor, I said nothing. I simply tried to keep my mind focused on getting home safely. And now that I've lived all these years and my heavenly Father has seen me through many a storm, I know he's able to take me all the way home if I just trust him. And when I enter a danger zone, I'm not naive.

THIRTY-SIX

Figure It Out for Yourself

One of the most sterling examples of someone who figured out life for himself is George Washington Carver. Born into poverty and slavery, his childhood was virtually unbearable. Nevertheless, he left us a legacy of gifts that are, by their sheer magnitude, almost unbelievable.

When George was a week old, slave night raiders kidnapped him. His owner hired someone to find him and get him back. In doing so, he was traded for a horse. George was taught to read and write by an unknown woman named "Aunt Susan" who imprinted into his memory this phrase: "You must learn all you can. Then go back out into the world and give your learning back to the people."

That's exactly what he did. Driven to get an education, he went to school through great hardship and learned all he could about every subject that came his way, winding up with a master's degree in agriculture and several honorary doctorates.

As if that were not enough, he was the recipient of awards of merit, and in 1952 *Popular Mechanics* selected him as one of fifty outstanding Americans. Coins and stamps were printed with his likeness. Museums were named after him. A movie was made in his honor, and he was inducted into the National Inventors Hall of Fame. My favorite recognition of George Washington Carver happened in 1941 when *Time* magazine dubbed him the "Black Leonardo" in reference to the great Renaissance inventor and artist Leonardo da Vinci.

His humility, humanitarianism, frugality, and good nature enabled the rest of us today to enjoy and benefit from his accomplishments in the fields of agricultural education, improvement in racial relations, mentoring children, painting, and writing poetry—one of which is entitled "Figure It Out for Yourself."

George Washington Carver didn't leave a stone unturned. In his seventy-nine years on earth as a slave, scientist, botanist, educator, inventor, and Christian (he invited Jesus Christ into his heart when he was ten), he's left a legacy of figuring out life in such a way that we find ourselves wanting to emulate his rejection of materialism and embrace his love of learning. Carver died in 1943, and on his tombstone are these words: "He could have added fortune to fame, but caring for neither, he found happiness and honor in being helpful to the world."

Figuring it out for oneself requires discipline. It asks us to observe a few simple, personal guidelines, such as having character matter more than reputation, knowing what we can control and

what we can't, learning that the good life is a life of inner seren-
ity, never suppressing generosity. It means living wisely. To figure
something out, we have to examine how things fit together. We all
come equipped with the same set of tools: a brain, a conscience, a
will, and a heart. With these tools, we look within our own souls
in order to understand what lies within the souls of others. And
our goal is to figure out what constitutes who we really are. We try
to establish common sense, to understand others and what they're
saying, to accept ourselves, and to figure out why we carry grudges
or make judgments. We learn from our mistakes. It may not be
easy, especially at first, but this is the most courageous way to live.

Because George Washington Carver was as interested in his
students' character development as he was in their intellectual
development, he lived by a list of eight virtues and taught them in
his classes. I'll leave you with those. As you think through them,
try to apply them in the days, months, and years ahead.

- Be clean both inside and out.
- Neither look up to the rich nor down on the poor.
- Lose, if need be, without squealing.
- Win without bragging.
- Always be considerate of women, children, and older people.
- Be too brave to lie.
- Be too generous to cheat.
- Take your share of the world and let others take theirs.

Remember this: as you figure out life for yourself, start doing
common things in an uncommon way. When you do, you'll command the attention of the world.

THIRTY-SEVEN

Discover What Makes People Tick

People fascinate me. I could sit on a park bench all day and strike up a conversation with anyone about anything: rich or poor, young or old, male or female. I'm not as interested in externals (Where'd you get that purse? Where are you flying today?) as I am in discovering what makes people tick. For me, discovering what powers someone's inner workings has been the pursuit of a lifetime.

It's equally fascinating to discover who we are, ourselves. Perhaps others define us as someone's sibling, wife, mother, grandmother, friend, neighbor, or employee, but who are we inside, walls down, roofs off? What makes us tick?

Proverbs 22:6 says, "Start children off on the way they should go, and even when they are old they will not turn from it" (NIV). That means children reared in the nurture and admonition of the Lord will be trained to follow him as they grow older. It doesn't mean they absolutely *will* follow him, but they've been trained to do so. It also means if they seek to live within the confines of their giftedness, or "bent," they'll more than likely *tick* in that direction.

Let's look at it this way: I have two very close friends who know each other well but are as different as daylight and dark regarding their individual inclinations. One is almost clairvoyant when it comes to the physical needs of others. She seems to know when to offer help, even when there's no request beforehand from the needy person. More often than not, my friend takes care of the need before it manifests itself. She can sense what should be done, and does it. Meeting the physical needs of others is basically what makes her tick.

The second friend has the ability to determine what action should be taken when it comes to psychological needs. She's a born counselor and was that way as a young girl. When she was a high school student all her girlfriends discussed problems with her regarding themselves, boyfriends, parents, neighbors—because she innately knew how to help them. It's as though she could have been a counselor at the age of fifteen. That innate ability was her bent. It made her tick.

I've spent many years getting to know what makes *me* tick. I've found it true what Viktor Frankl said: "The creation of personal meaning is central to a satisfying life." Discovering what makes me tick has helped me see and understand the inclinations that make others tick as well.

I suggest you get to know what makes *you* tick by asking yourself a few simple questions:

- *What is important to me?* Write down a list of essential and meaningful attributes or activities in your life in the order of value. I did this a few years ago, and I look at it now and then to see if these same things still matter. They do.
- *Do I lead with my head or my heart?* Take time to analyze how decisions are made, and once they're made, determine what is to be done next. Keep a good balance between what needs to be done and how you feel about it after it's done.
- *How do I treat other people?* This is a very important question. On your answer hinges your belief system, behavior, and reputation. There's no substitute for kindness and grace in daily living. It says volumes about who you are.
- *Do my actions harmonize with my way of life?* This is not so much what you do but how you do it. When you understand this and live by this principle, inner peace will be possible even if hard times come. Don't make up your own rules. Seek harmony.
- *Who is the person I want to be?* Determine your goals and ideals. Determine who you admire and why. Don't be vague. Learn to define who you are with only yourself in the definition.

I encourage you to spend time by yourself, getting to know yourself. It's been said that people who celebrate solitude make the most contributions to humankind. Solitude gives clarity and enlightenment, and those two attributes help you discover who you are and who others are as well.

THIRTY-EIGHT

Fight Resentment Before It Festers

For years I held a grudge against a friend. It was a long time ago, but I well remember the feelings of that pain. I carried the grudge with me wherever I went, and it was a slow-eating cancer in my soul.

After much conviction and many tears, I finally poured out my broken, self-centered heart to God and asked him to forgive me and help me clean up the cesspool of resentment I had carried around too long. And he did. It was slow and tedious at first because of my stubborn will, but I can say without a shadow of a doubt that God healed me. When I stopped wanting to get revenge and reached out for God's forgiveness, everything changed, and I learned some of life's most important lessons.

The Greek philosopher Epictetus once said, "One of the signs of the dawning of moral progress is the gradual extinguishing of blame." I believe it. The minute I started taking my eyes off my own rotten attitude and turned them to a forgiving God, the blame game stopped. There was no resentment left.

I've asked myself a thousand times why I didn't fight that resentment before it became a festering pool in my spirit. I was a fool to wait. I was immature. I wanted the other person to suffer because of the grudge I carried. I really believe it's as simple as that.

Have you ever found yourself in that boat? You probably have. Rare is the individual who can go through life without feeling resentment, harboring a grudge, or blaming somebody else for an offense. And seemingly the only way for that not to happen is to fight resentment before it has time to fester and become a boil on the surface of a relationship. This is what it takes to win that FIGHT:

- Figure out what went wrong and determine to seek resolution.
- Initiate a conversation with the person who has offended you.
- Get feedback, then give your interpretation of what that means.
- Hear ideas for discussion without being stubborn.
- Together, seek clarity, understanding, and forgiveness.

Nobody knows better than I do that this is not easy. One of the hardest things in the world is to forgive somebody who has wronged us. But there are countless Scriptures on the value of forgiveness, and God makes doing it possible. I can tell you from experience, if we put it off because we fear confrontation or deny the offense ever happened, it will get bigger and bigger. It will fester.

I hate confrontation and will do almost anything in the world to avoid it, but I've learned from the school of hard knocks, if we gently confront someone about an issue that separates us, it pays off in the end. Once the rift is healed, there is peace, calm, and gratitude like you've never felt before.

After the situation got better between my friend and me I remember reading in Matthew 5:22–24 these convicting words from Jesus: "This is how I want you to conduct yourself in these matters. If you enter your place of worship and, about to make an offering, you suddenly remember a grudge a friend has against you, abandon your offering, leave immediately, go to this friend and make things right. Then and only then, come back and work things out with God."

I also believe this verse applies to the one holding the grudge, not just the one against whom the grudge is held. As I read it, I was reminded again of how we can undermine ourselves when we allow something this detrimental to decay in our spirits. But when we ask for forgiveness and *mean* it, we open ourselves up to the God of the universe, who not only forgives but also teaches us how to forgive others.

Matthew 6:14–15 says, "In prayer there is a connection between what God does and what you do. You can't get forgiveness from God, for instance, without also forgiving others. If you refuse to do your part, you cut yourself off from God's part."

{ THIRTY-NINE }

Cook Something
Special for Yourself

Half my life has been lived in small, rented apartments when money was tight. I learned to make do with what was at hand. I had to be creative about clothes, furnishings, gifts, and meals. And certainly about travel—when I was able to go anywhere, that is.

Now that I look back on those years from the vantage point of a debt-free homeowner, I have to say those were some of the best and most enjoyable years of my life. There's something about being in a small space, with little to work with, that makes one's creative juices flow. Truly, necessity is the mother of invention.

One of the ways I enjoyed those years was spending time in the kitchen. My mother was a fantastic cook, and she taught me some of the tricks of the trade. Because so much of my life has been spent alone, I learned to cook special things just for myself and build a whole evening around the meal.

For example, every December I would set aside a night that was just for my out-of-town friends and me. Of course, none of them could be there in person, but they might as well have been because the entire evening was devoted to being with them. We exchanged gifts, by mail, and I opened their gifts under the Christmas tree and then called each one after his or her gift was unwrapped. We talked, laughed, caught up on each other's lives, and had a wonderful visit about the gift I'd been given. I called that annual celebration "my very own Christmas party," and one of its highlights was the meal. I would cook most of the day in preparation for the evening, making some delectable dish for myself.

One year I made a recipe from the "centerfold" of *Gourmet* magazine. Of course, I had lots of leftovers, which I enjoyed for days to come. I still laugh about it because a little part of the kitchen caught on fire when the recipe got out of hand. But I managed to put out the flame almost as fast as it started. Now it's a laughable moment in my memory bank.

Unfortunately, lots of people simply don't want to cook if they don't have others eating with them. They open a can and throw some unappetizing concoction together just to get through the grind of having to fix a meal. They ask themselves, *Who needs the mess? Why dirty the pots and pans and do all this work just for me?*

If you do that, you're missing the joy of cooking something special for yourself, as well as the possibility of having a creative adventure in the kitchen. On the other hand, when you're willing to step out on the edge a little, you might find recipes that will not only please your palate and your pocketbook but also provide you with a fun story for your memory bank (in case you set *your* kitchen on fire).

I had a delicious meal at an Italian restaurant in Los Angeles one night and wanted to repeat that pasta recipe for myself. So I called the restaurant and asked to speak to the chef. Not only did he come to the phone, but he gladly told me the ingredients and exactly how to cook the pasta. I was absolutely *thrilled*. As he walked me through the whole thing step by step, I made the recipe. Now and then he excused himself from the phone to answer various questions from his waiters. Not only did I have a wonderful pasta dish for dinner that night, but I've also cooked that recipe dozens of times since then, and it's become a favorite of friends who've eaten around my table.

"Cooking is my *kinderspiel*," said Wolfgang Puck, "my child's play. You can make it yours too. And while you're cooking, don't forget to share and laugh. Laugh a great deal, and with much love— it enhances the flavor of the food."

Don't hold back from cooking something time-consuming or difficult for yourself simply because you feel like it's too much work for one person or that people might wonder why you go to the trouble. Sing while you cook. Rehearse your Bible verses. Pray. Talk to the food. Have fun, and write about it in your journal when the meal's over. There'll always be people who don't understand why you do what you do. But quite honestly, if you knew the truth, they might be wishing they were more like you.

⸭ **FORTY** ⸭

Celebrate the
Life You're Given

Not long ago, I read Eric Metaxas's biography of Dietrich Bonhoeffer, and I don't know when I've appreciated a book more. Everything about Bonhoeffer's life had meaning and purpose, from his child-hood till the day of his martyrdom at the hand of Nazi officers in 1945. In every sense of the word, he celebrated the life he was given. He loved his family, friends, work, ministry, art, music, literature, theater, travel, learning, teaching, and studying different cultures from all over the world.

Bonhoeffer gave his life away to encourage and bless others, no matter the cost. He was a gentleman to the core and a dedi-cated Christian. Even during his years of imprisonment, he didn't complain; he loved his enemies and prayed for them daily. His confidence was not in his circumstances but in the Lord Jesus Christ.

One of the many inspiring things Bonhoeffer wrote was this remarkable thought: "The right to live is a matter of essence, not values. In the sight of God there is no life that is not worth living. . . . The fact that God is the Creator, Preserver, and Redeemer of life makes even the most wretched life worth living before God."

The words "the right to live is a matter of essence, not values" caught my attention, and I've continued to think about them since I first read them. Bonhoeffer believed that each of us lives and has our being, and that's what enables us to celebrate. He was saying the value of our lives is not predicated on who we are or when and where we were born. The worth or value of one's life is inherent in every human being—it's in the fact that we are simply alive in the first place. Being alive is enough in itself to give us reason to celebrate.

But sometimes it doesn't seem so. It's easy for us to think our lives and even our worth can be measured by the number of degrees behind our name, the money in our bank account, the languages we speak, and the heads that turn when we enter a room. We can easily bypass the reality that life itself is the gift God gives us. It matters. We matter. And, quite honestly, *that's* what matters. Think about it.

What is more important than the fact that you have breath in your lungs? Is accomplishment more important? While that's both satisfying and profitable, is it more important? Is accumulation? The people we know? Where we go? What we think of ourselves? What others think of us? Or is the value of your life in the "essence" of you, as Bonhoeffer wrote?

As I read this perspective of Bonhoeffer's, I thought of my own father, who had a stroke when he was in his late eighties. It almost killed him and left him very frail and faltering. His level of activity, speech, and lifestyle changed, but the "essence" of him didn't change. Who he was remained the same before and after the stroke. He remained exceedingly generous, giving away what he had.

The day before Daddy died in a nursing home, I went to see him (not knowing, of course, that would be our last visit). I took him a Hershey bar, his favorite treat. He asked me to unwrap it for him, which I did. Then, without hesitation, he offered it to me and then to the man with whom he shared a room. Next he offered it to the nurse, to the doctor, and to passers-by in the hall. By the time the bar got back to Daddy, there were only two little squares left.

"I only wanted a taste," he said. Then he looked at me and said, "Thank you, honey. Just having you with me is sweeter than this candy bar anyway. I so appreciate your coming. You look beautiful."

Bonhoeffer was right. God's value, as well as yours and mine, is in our essence—that which is inside us, that which God has redeemed and will live forever.

{ PART FIVE }

Staying Connected

FORTY-ONE

Listen with Your Whole Heart

I come from a verbal family. More often than not, everybody talked at once. If I were to step back into that childhood scene, knowing what I know now, I'm sure I'd be surprised at all the noise. We three kids were certainly made to obey our parents, but I don't remember anything being said about the importance of listening. It seemed everybody was eager to be heard, but nobody was eager to listen. Maybe your home was like that too.

I remember reading somewhere that there are two kinds of bores: those who talk too much and those who listen too little. That was our family in a nutshell. It wasn't until I was grown that I realized I'd probably been boring people into a coma for years.

Now that I've lived a long time and changed some of my bad habits into good ones, I've learned how to listen, and now I realize it's an art form. Generally speaking, these days I prefer listening to talking. When a few rules are followed, anybody can become a good listener, and when those rules are kept, one can easily practice it.

Listening with your whole heart takes concentration and focus. Here's what works for me: look directly at the person talking and don't interrupt. If you're afraid you're going to forget something important you want to say, jot down a quick word so you can refer to it later. Keep an open mind to the facts being shared without judging actions or behavior.

Along the road of life, I was blessed to have friends who cared enough about me to model these rules and pass along helpful pointers. But maybe my best listening teacher has been Proverbs 20:5. That verse has helped me immensely, both in listening to others and in having them listen to me. I like to see how it's presented in two different versions of the Bible, first in the New King James Version, and then in *The Message*:

> Counsel in the heart of man is like deep water, but a man of understanding will draw it out.

> Knowing what is right is like deep water in the heart; a wise person draws from the well within.

Picture two people talking. One is the person with the counsel in his or her heart and the other is the person of understanding. As the first person talks, the second one listens. But where is the counsel? It's in the heart of the first person, not in the one who is listening.

So often when we're the listener, we feel like we have to give our counsel, our opinion, our judgment in response to what's being said. But all that counsel lies in the heart of the one talking. The listener just draws it out. He extends an empty bucket of kindness and questions down into that heart and gently draws out what the other person needs to know that is already there. As the listener, it's not our job to point out what should be done. It's our job to receive, encourage, occasionally ask pertinent questions, and simply listen. As the talker processes his or her thoughts aloud and the listener receives those thoughts, the counsel will come from inside the one talking. And if the "man of understanding" doesn't listen, no progress will be made.

Undoubtedly, the thing we all want when somebody listens to us is to be understood and valued. We shut up the minute we're judged. Remember this: we're only open to the degree we are received. We want to be heard by one who cares about us and listens to what we have to say. Are you that person? Am I? That's the question we need to ask ourselves.

The golden rule of friendship is to listen to others—as you would have them listen to you.

{ FORTY-TWO }

Communicate Often with Loved Ones

The first time I met the members of Hawk Nelson, a Christian rock band from Canada, I loved them immediately. Not only are they talented musicians, but they're also warm and friendly. Even though they're decades younger than I, they're welcoming and thoughtful in every respect. But the most impressive thing to me was when lead vocalist Jason Dunn told me how much he loved his mother and called her every day.

I was *stunned*. Here he is in his twenties, and he knows what it means to a mother to hear from her son often. So he calls her every day.

How cool is that? When I see him from time to time now at

conferences, my standard question is, "Have you called your mother today?"

Sometimes before I even open my mouth, he greets me with a big smile and says, "Yes, Luci. I've called her."

Some people might think it's way too much for a twenty-something young man who's married to put in a daily call to his mom. They'd view that as being a "momma's boy," but I can tell you he's anything but. He's simply thoughtful to someone he loves.

One of the nicest things we can do for our loved ones is to call them or contact them in some other personal way. Most people live busy lives, and that busyness keeps them from reaching out to their loved ones. But it doesn't have to be that way. There are lots of avenues, especially in today's world, to communicate with those we care about. It's almost mind-boggling the number of ways we can keep in contact with people now.

Personally, I loved the days of letter writing, and I was good at it. Anybody remember those days? That's when you actually took a piece of stationery and composed a letter to somebody by hand, put a stamp on the envelope, and took it to the mailbox. Of course, being a packrat, I have most of the letters I ever received—boxes and boxes of them. In fact, when a friend of mine died about twelve years ago, her family gave me back the 107 postcards I'd written her during our friendship. She had saved them all, and her loved ones saw to it that I got them. I'm sure they knew I'd treasure them as much as she had. I *love* postcards and have collected them from friends all over the world. It's a quick and loving way to touch base.

I have to admit, though, perhaps my most prized possessions in terms of communication are the forty-seven letters from my brother, Chuck Swindoll, that he wrote me during his time in the Marine Corps in the 1950s (especially when he was stationed on the island of Okinawa). To me, those letters are pure gold. Many of them refer to his relationship with the Lord and his desire to go into public Christian ministry. They're part of his foundational thoughts for where he is today, which is right here in the Dallas area, where he works as a pastor, head of Insight for Living radio ministry, and chancellor of Dallas Theological Seminary.

I love looking back on all the years we've stayed in touch through letters, phone calls, reunions, ministry, birthdays, family gatherings, texts, and now e-mails. I know people who don't even know where their siblings are, and here I am with one of my sweet brothers living just a few blocks from me. We were pals when we tossed the football in the backyard of our little Swindoll house in Houston, and we've laughed together on fishing trips with Mother and Daddy. I sang in his wedding more than fifty years ago and said good-bye to him at the airport when he went off to military duty. I witnessed his graduation from DTS and his becoming president at that same school thirty-two years later. And now, every Sunday I'm home and not at a conference somewhere, I hear him preach at Stonebriar Community Church in Frisco and often have lunch with him after the service.

Did I know we would wind up as neighbors, spending our final years together in rich fellowship? Of course not. Neither of us planned this, but we've stayed close all our lives because we love each other. Being neighbors now is one of those surprising gifts of God's grace.

If you've lost contact with family members or friends, don't put off getting in touch with them. You never know how your life will be enriched by reestablishing those relationships. Job 5:8 says God is "famous for great and unexpected acts; there's no end to his surprises." Staying in communication with your loved ones—or reconnecting with them—pays off, folks. Don't miss those surprises God has in store for you. Pay attention to the little things God does, especially those for which you've never asked. Then thank him and tell somebody you love what he's done for you.

{ FORTY-THREE }

Set the Table for Company

The French gastronome A. Brillat-Savarin once said, "To invite a person into your house is to take charge of his happiness for as long as he is under your roof." That was my mother's philosophy. In spite of our family's small quarters, she rolled out the red carpet for guests: courtesy was extended at the door, soft music came from the radio, the best chair in the house was offered, a meal was prepared, and the table was set to perfection. Unless we were having a picnic, I can't even remember a time when our little dining table was not set for a family meal. We had no television, so nobody ate off a TV tray. Everybody came to the table when called, and a blessing was said before we ate. Long after my mother had passed away, a friend said to me one day, "Your mother was so civilized." Indeed she was.

To my mother, setting a beautiful table often expressed more love to the family and guests than the food we were about to eat. It showed thoughtfulness, care, and attention to details. Mother, in her simple way, was a lot like Brillat-Savarin. In his book *The Physiology of Taste* (first published in 1825 and still in print today), he tells us that even the simplest meal pleased him if it was executed with artistry.

In many ways, I've inherited Mother's love of beauty and the value of artistry when setting a table for company. She put a great deal of emphasis on the dishes and silverware being in the right spot, napkins folded just so, and the guest or guests seated at a place of honor. Today I do the same.

When I was a senior in college in 1955, my mother began painting a set of china for my graduation gift. I still have that sixty-piece set with orange blossoms painted all over the cups, saucers, plates, and bowls. Even as I sit here writing this chapter, those dishes are displayed in a china cabinet about twenty feet away that I designed and had especially built to show off Mother's gorgeous gift. She signed and dated each piece. When I look at those dishes now, I'm reminded again of the time and love it took to complete that project. Mother died forty years ago, so I treasure this gift more with each passing year.

From time to time, I throw a dinner party. With the care I inherited from Mother, I set my long table in the library. Not only do I use my best dishes and the silver utensils she gave me, but I also make place cards for every guest and have a flower arrangement as the centerpiece. In my spare time, I work on that table for days on end, starting early with the place cards that are representative of the season or the reason for the party. I've made cards from beads, balls, birds, baskets, and balloons. I've copied quotations or Scriptures to fit each person, drawn pictures of animals and children, and cut apart maps and folded paper to make model airplanes, toys, hats, and bracelets. We've had treasure hunts at the table, and at times I've handed out sheet music so we could all sing together in harmony. I always enjoy making these efforts because I want the guests around my table to remember a meal that's fun and different.

Does this take time? Of course. Does it require going the extra mile? Yes. Have I ever said I'll never do this again? Just the opposite!

Next time you throw a dinner party or invite guests to share a holiday meal or even when you prepare a weekday family meal, do something out of the ordinary. Use the best of what you have and set the table for company. Not that you have to have expensive china or silver. You don't even have to have a dining room. Just make the kitchen table look special with some kind of attractive centerpiece. Serve a delicious meal. Talk and laugh a lot. Take pictures. Make a memory. Then, if you've invited guests, say good-bye with love and kisses and God's blessings on those who have to leave. You won't regret a single moment you spent making the occasion special. Brillat-Savarin also said, "The pleasure of the table belongs to all ages, to all countries, and to all areas; it mingles with all other pleasures, and remains at last to console us for their departure."

I predict that you'll find you don't have to spend a lot of money on the extra details that go into setting the table for company. It's the love and care for your guests that your gesture shows.

FORTY-FOUR

Trust Friends for the Truth

Some of my closest friends are shrinks. Or they've had therapy with one. Personally, I love people who've had therapy and think like therapists. The way they reason interests me, and their viewpoint of mental and emotional challenges helps me look at life through another lens.

One of the things I value most about these therapeutic friends is that I can count on them to tell me the truth, which in my view, is exceedingly important in friendship. If my friends won't be honest with me, who will? And since I've been single all my life, some of my friends are as close to me as members of my family. In some ways they know more about me than the people I grew up with because we've been together on a daily basis for most of my adult years.

Sometimes I don't really like the truth they tell me, but even when I don't, I almost always come around and eventually accept what they say. Here's why: they know *how* to say it.

You see, there's a catch to the value of truth telling: it's all in how it's told. Of course we need to know the truth about ourselves, but remember this from chapter 41: We have to be really willing to *listen* and *receive* the truth that's being shared with us. If the truth hurts us, we're inclined to back away. As the prophet wrote in Amos 5:10, "Raw truth is never popular."

Instead of feeding something "raw" to the hearer, why not cook it a bit on the back burner of our hearts before offering it to someone else? Couch what you have to say in gentleness. I'm not saying you should beat around the bush; simply be mindful that what you're saying could be hurtful. Make sure it doesn't sound angry or accusatory.

And if you're the one hearing the truth, receive it as something that probably took courage to say, and appreciate your friend's honesty. It might be that he or she felt brave enough to speak the truth to you only because your relationship is strong enough to allow it.

In my close circle of friends, we have a somewhat unspoken rule that we'll be up front with each other. Because our community is a "sisterhood" and we all live near one another geographically, we try very hard to stay current and sensitive when it comes to each other's feelings. Sometimes it can be painful to hear the truth we need to know. But in our circle—and I imagine in yours too—truth has to be told to keep communication open. Not being truthful causes more harm than good.

Eight years ago, when I was building my home, a neighbor helped me make decisions regarding the tile, brick, and trim I wanted to use. Together we went to the design center to select the right colors and textures, but, as I mentioned earlier, because I had to travel so much during those days and she didn't, she volunteered to oversee a lot of the construction when I couldn't be on the premises.

One day while I was out of town she and I had a little disagreement on the phone. She discovered the workmen were putting the wrong color on the window trim, and she wanted to represent me in telling them to change the color to what I had initially chosen. Knowing that would delay the process, after a few exchanges back and forth, I told her we'd just stay with the color they were using. "After all, it's my house," I said curtly.

I was perfectly willing to let it go, thinking it didn't matter that much in the end, but she was not. She kept saying it wouldn't be that hard to change and I would like it better when all was said and done.

I grew frustrated because I felt she was trying to "run my business." Oh, brother! I knew at some point we would have to talk about the issue. Hating confrontation, I dreaded that encounter.

When I got home, my friend kindly asked if we could look at the problem together. Reluctantly, I said yes. She carefully and truthfully spelled out her side of the story. Appreciating her gentle manner and her desire to make it right, I confessed my stubbornness and my bad attitude when I had talked with her on the phone. I asked her to forgive me. At the end of our conversation, she suggested we pray together. In that prayer she thanked the Lord for helping us both to be transparent.

Because of my friend's kindness and her genuine effort to get to the truth of the matter, I was reminded again of Proverbs 24:26: "An honest answer is like a warm hug."

I love the way my brother Chuck put it when he said, "Honesty has a beautiful and refreshing simplicity about it. No ulterior motives. No hidden meanings. An absence of hypocrisy, duplicity, political games, and verbal superficiality. As honesty and real integrity characterize our lives, there will be no need to manipulate others."

{ **FORTY-FIVE** }

Forgive Others
Over and Over

Several years ago I frequented a particular flower shop owned by a horticulturalist. He told me that when his grandfather died, he left him a plot of land in his will so the boy could grow plants and have a nursery. He also said the grandfather had done the same thing for my friend's older brother. The older brother, however, was given a greater portion of the land than he. After three years of disagreement between them, their mother sided with the younger son and the father with the older. Ultimately, what was to have been a gift became such a point of contention that the two sides wouldn't speak to each other. It was a full-fledged family feud.

When I first heard this story, I have to say my response was disbelief. One day while at the flower shop I was talking with the owner, and I said to him, "Do you ever think about sitting down with your brother and making amends? Might you ever forgive one another? What was meant to be a gift has become such a burden; forgiveness might make you both feel better."

"Forgive?" he asked, looking inquisitively. "I will never forgive him. Forgiveness is a myth, and it doesn't work. I'd rather carry a grudge than forgive him. I want what's mine, and I plan to get it."

I decided to drop the issue and ultimately stopped going to the shop. Frankly, the presence of that spirit made me uncomfortable. There were other places to buy flowers, and I simply found myself choosing to go elsewhere. Lack of forgiveness for his brother was destroying this man, and every time I was in his presence, I could feel it more and more.

The Bible tells us to "forgive one another as quickly and thoroughly as God in Christ forgave you" (Ephesians 4:32). Of course, that's much easier said than done. When we've been offended, something in us wants to get even. Some of us have a veritable mineshaft of grudges and offenses we've carried for years, and nothing is going to stop us from retaliating.

I've now lived long enough to tell you from experience that this kind of bitterness and rancor will eat you alive. If you let it happen, your heart will harden, and without an open heart, there will be no way for the Holy Spirit to do his work of healing because the one who's been wounded will lick, feed, and nurture that wound. As a result, the hardness intensifies until it is far beyond the hard-heartedness of the one who caused the offense; it reaches a stage where a simple apology would never do. It's too late for that.

Yet even in that situation, the only solution is to forgive. Forgiveness wipes the slate clean. Instead of rubbing it in when we've been hurt, we must learn to rub it out. Forgiveness is much more important to the one who does the forgiving than to the one who is being forgiven. Healing starts when we forgive. An open heart heals much more easily. God can work in a heart that's open.

We have all failed. Made mistakes. Said and done stupid things. Be that as it may, life goes on, and we must go with it. Those who give and forgive are the richest people in the world. They've accepted their inadequacies and shortcomings and have learned to forgive others over and over. And in so doing, they can forgive themselves.

I have no idea what finally became of the two brothers. But when I think of them, I'm reminded of these lines from Alfred Lord Tennyson:

> *Two aged men, that had been foes for life,*
> *Met by a grave, and wept—And in those tears*
> *They washed away the memory of their strife:*
> *Then wept again the loss of all those years.*

Perhaps this is what happened with the two brothers whose relationship was broken by a gift.

{ FORTY-SIX }

Invite People to Your Home

One of my close friends comes from a family of eight children. When she was growing up, it was the custom in her family to invite school chums over for meals, to spend the night or, on occasion, the weekend. Their mother thought nothing of it if there were ten or twelve kids at the dinner table instead of the usual eight. On the other hand, because there were so many in the family, they were never invited out, so their mother had an open-door policy for friends. It was the norm. She never objected; she was such a gracious and hospitable woman, she made it a point to see that nobody known by her family was left out if he or she needed a meal, a bed to sleep in, or a place to stay.

I was amused when my friend told me she was attending the funeral of her older sister many years later, and in the crowd of those who had gathered, there was a gentleman she knew but couldn't quite place in her mind. She asked him to refresh her memory.

"I was your brother Phil's friend. He was wonderful to me. In fact, I don't know if you remember this or not, but I lived with your family for a year. I had no place to stay, so Phil asked me to live there. I'm not sure your mother ever knew it. I just sort of joined the crowd and was considered part of the family. I loved it."

When I was told that story, I laughed out loud. Not so much because it's humorous, but because of the joy it must have been for that young man to live in a home like that, where no questions were asked about how many were at the table, sleeping over, having fun with the kids. Perhaps without knowing it, this woman has been practicing what the apostle Paul encourages us to do in Romans 12:13: "Be inventive in hospitality."

Hospitality is a state of mind. It's having a spirit of giving and caring. We're told throughout Scripture to be hospitable, but unfortunately, it's rapidly becoming a lost art. Nobody has time anymore—or takes time. Life goes too fast. Inviting people to one's home is a luxury—and who takes time for luxury these days?

When I talk about hospitality, I always think of my older brother, Orville, and his wife, Erma Jean. They are classic examples of those who have invited people to their home all their married lives. And they still do it now, even though they're in their eighties.

Orville and E. J. spent the majority of their lives as missionaries in Argentina. But no matter where they live, there has rarely been a time they didn't have someone else living with them or spending a week or so with them. Their friends have left luggage or belongings there while doing mission work in the area. I so commend them for their extensive outreach of hospitality. It speaks volumes of love and grace. The welcome mat is always out.

They now live in Miami, but they seldom have a weekend when someone isn't visiting, having a meal with them, holding a meeting in their home, or sharing an evening together with them. Their friends are all over the world, and those friends know full well when they come to (or through) Miami, they're welcome at the Swindoll home—day or night, breakfast or dinner, alone or with family members. They model 3 John 1:5: "When you extend hospitality to Christian brothers and sisters, even when they are strangers, you make the faith visible."

Neither of these families, my friend's or Orville's, waited until everything was perfect to practice hospitality. They started the minute they had a home, as simple and unassuming as it might have been. People often think they'll have guests over when they get new flooring in the kitchen. Then it's when they get new carpet, then a new sofa, and then a bigger patio. It never ends. Don't let life pass you by because the placemats don't match. Reach out. Share stories. Laugh together. Create memories. Make your faith visible.

{ **FORTY-SEVEN** }

Share the Bread of Life

For more than sixteen years, I've been a speaker with Women of Faith. Every year I travel to about fifteen cities and speak to about two hundred thousand women. The irony is that I've never wanted to be in ministry. I didn't like the word. To "do ministry" meant I had to dress up, go somewhere, talk to somebody about sin in her life, and then set her straight with the gospel. (Or at least, that was my thinking.) I felt like people who engaged in ministry were called to preach. Or teach. All I wanted to do was enjoy life. Besides, I have two brothers who have been in public Christian ministry since their twenties. *That's enough for one family*, I thought.

I was reared in a Christian home where studying the Bible was emphasized, prayer was encouraged, forgiveness was practiced, and reverence for all things spiritual was taught. And I believed it.

At the age of ten, during Vacation Bible School at our little church down the road from our house, I accepted Jesus Christ as my Savior. My grandmother was my VBS teacher and explained how to pray a prayer of faith, and having done that, I became a Christian. That was enough for me.

But when I grew up, started going to Bible classes, and learned about the depth, width, and breadth of God's Word, I was truly amazed, and my life changed in every way. I realized I could live a grace-filled life as opposed to one controlled by legalism. I was introduced to theological doctrine that counseled and taught me the truth about the Trinity: God the Father, God the Son, and God the Holy Spirit. I learned to look at life from God's viewpoint rather than my own. I learned Jesus Christ loves me just as I am.

In short, I learned about the Bread of Life, and I wanted to share that knowledge with everybody by the way I lived, loved, learned—and enjoyed life. Jesus says in John 6:35–38:

> I am the Bread of Life. The person who aligns with me hungers no more and thirsts no more, ever. I have told you this explicitly because even though you have seen me in action, you don't really believe me. Every person the Father gives me eventually comes running to me. And once that person is with me, I hold on and don't let go. I came down from heaven not to follow my own whim but to accomplish the will of the One who sent me.

When I became acquainted with that verse, I ran to Jesus Christ, and he's never let me go; I've found constant nourishment in this Bread.

And when I finally figured out the importance of doctrine, I saw that God was basically in the business of two things: bringing those who don't know him as their Savior to knowledge of himself, and bringing those who know him to maturity in their faith.

When we believe we have sinned and come short of the glory of God and invite Jesus Christ into our hearts, he comes in, lives there, and fills us with his Spirit. That action of belief is when God declares us righteous, while we are still in our sinning state. We don't deserve it; nevertheless, by grace he gives us forgiveness, peace, purpose, and redemption in a moment of time. That is called *justification*. It happens once and for all time; once it happens, we are justified forever and ever. That will never change.

Becoming mature in Christ is very different. It will take the rest of our lives. It involves tests, challenges, growth, setbacks, waiting, trusting, disappointments, and so forth. All the things we go through to grow up as a human being. That is called *sanctification*. It will go on until we are taken in death, to live in eternity with God.

They are complicated-sounding words, but they're easy to understand. Look at it this way:

- What we are in Christ never changes: *justification*.
- Who we are in Christ never stops changing: *sanctification*.

Knowing and believing this truth is by far the greatest gift you can give yourself—and then give to others. It's a matter of faith, and once it's inside you, it becomes your ministry—whether you want it to be or not! You are carrying around the Bread of Life, and how you live *your* life has the capacity to feed people who are starving to death and don't even know it.

Enjoy life—and live generously!

{ FORTY-EIGHT }

Support Your Community with Love

In all the years I've lived on this earth, all the communities I've shared with friends, all the neighbors who have showered me with love and help, one of the best examples I know of is a guy named Pat. My friends and I call him Pat the Handyman. And that title really fits him.

There seems to be nothing he can't do. We call him day or night, rain or shine, sick or well, and his response is always the same: "Piece o' cake. I'll be right there." And he means it. Even though he's married with a family and lives a few miles away, within a short time, his car rounds the corner, and he's on the front porch, ready to take care of the problem or meet the need. I'm convinced this guy can do everything but walk on water, and frankly, I've wondered if he does that, too, behind closed doors.

For example, he's come to my house and hung pictures, polished silver, brought groceries, cleaned my garage, repaired a broken chair, rewired a lamp, and fixed my garage door. At my friends' home, he's taken down Christmas decorations, caulked sinks, carried boxes to the attic, turned mattresses, driven them to the airport or the doctor, planted trees, worked on cars, cleaned patios, swept off porches, repaired toilets, unstopped sinks, and fed the dog.

But here's my favorite thing about Pat: he never complains. Never. Nothing is ever *too much* or takes *too long*. It's his spirit. He's even called my friends and me out of the blue to ask if we need something lifted, painted, lugged, mowed, started, or stopped. And there has never been a time he's asked for a penny. More often than not, he tries to refuse payment by saying, "Hey, I was down the street anyway. You don't need to pay me for this."

A couple of weeks ago I asked if he could pick up my mail when I had a five-day out-of-town commitment.

"Piece o' cake."

When I got home, the mail was all sorted in a bag and placed in a basket awaiting my return. I had to actually track the man down to pay him for that service. Oh, my gosh! Why don't we have more people like Pat? He's the kind of person you want as a neighbor, a helper, a friend, a companion, and an employee. When I'm around him, Pat makes me want to be a better person and a better Christian. I find myself wanting to help everybody on my street and in my neighborhood. He models what the apostle Paul says in Galatians 5:13: "Use your freedom to serve one another in love." (And I just know somewhere in the Greek Paul must have added, "with no strings attached.")

If we were all supportive of one another like this, I'd bet my bottom dollar there would be fewer conflicts and hurt feelings. And a lot less one-upmanship. Kindness breeds kindness, and teamwork breeds teamwork. If somebody on your block needs a helping hand, why don't you be the first one to volunteer out of sheer love for life and for what God has done for you? Have fun with it and make it memorable by not asking for pay. Just smile and say it was a "piece o' cake."

{ FORTY-NINE }

Give Your Time, Energy, Money

When I got up this morning, I took a shower, washed my hair, threw on my sweats, rode my stationary bike, had breakfast, and then sat down at my desk to write a check for the electric bill. A few minutes later it hit me: within a couple of hours, I had spent every commodity I have in my power: time, energy, and money.

Have you ever stopped to think about how you spend *your* resources? All day long, right and left, we spend—rarely stopping to consider what's being spent. We're just trying to live our lives in a way that'll keep us going and not wear us out or break the bank. More often than not, we live our lives in all-about-*me* mode: all the duties I have to accomplish, all the meetings I have to attend, all the children I have to take care of, all the bills I have to pay, all the hours I have to work, all the pleasures I have to forfeit. When was the last time you thought about giving all that time, energy, and money to helping somebody else?

For example, I called a friend yesterday, hoping we could have coffee together. Turns out she was exceedingly busy filling out forms for a medical exam she has to take next week, so I asked her how (or if) I could help. She said, "There's nothing you can do, really. I need to hurriedly finish this, take care of several e-mails, talk to my niece on the phone, and be dressed to walk out the door in about thirty minutes for a meeting. I really need gas in my car but have no time to go to the service station."

Bingo! There was my green light. I couldn't help her with any of those other things because they concerned only her, but I could certainly help with getting gas in her car. So I told her I'd be there in ten minutes. I drove to her house, parked, got the keys to her car, drove to the gas pump, and filled it with gas. And I simply loved doing it. I'm crazy about this person and wanted to help, so I gave what I had in one fell swoop: time, energy, and money. Done.

By the same token, two weeks before, that same friend knew I needed a few groceries, and my arthritic knee was acting up, so I kept putting off going to the store. Unbeknownst to me, she went for me: got two bags of the groceries I usually buy, brought them to my house, and put them in my refrigerator just to help me. She gave me the gift of her time, energy, and money. Done.

One of the simplest secrets to having a happy life is to give your own life away. That may sound ironic to you, but I'm telling the truth. Unfortunately, when it comes to giving, lots of people come up empty. Empty-handed, that is. Literally. They give nothing. Please don't let that be you.

Giving can be expressed in a thousand different ways; it doesn't have to involve money: making a phone call, mowing the grass, cleaning somebody's house, babysitting, driving your car for a change when you go somewhere with a friend, picking up the tab, visiting someone in the hospital, phoning home, spending time with your family. We know all these things. I don't need to be naming them for you. They're basic. And they're universal. But are we giving? Or are we asking *why* we should give?

Author Os Guinness answers that question, "We give because we've been given to."

I would encourage you to start giving now if you aren't giving already. Sure, a million excuses can cross your mind, everything from "my bunions hurt" or "my show is on" to "later, when the kids are older" or "later, when I retire." I've heard it all. And none of it stands the test of good reasoning.

First Corinthians 12:5–6 says, "Each person is given something to do that shows who God is: Everyone gets in on it, everyone benefits." Imagine being a part of something that shows who God is. *That person can be you.*

Keep this as your motto and start today. I promise you, it will make all the difference in your life: "Blessed are those who can give without remembering and receive without forgetting."

{ **FIFTY** }

Live an Attitude
of Gratitude

Several weeks ago I ran across a note I had written my grandmother
when I was eight years old, thanking her for a sweater she'd given
me. With it was a letter to my father written when I was in college,
thanking him for sending me ten dollars to buy a book I'd wanted.
Wonder why I saved those notes? Maybe it's because I'm a packrat
at heart, or maybe it's because I just love thank you notes. Probably
both. When my brothers and I were children, we were taught to put
in writing our expressions of appreciation to our relatives, teachers, and friends. We still do it to this day.

A month or so ago, I gave both brothers copies of the big Eric
Metaxas book *Bonhoeffer*, a five-hundred-page tome that covers

every inch of Dietrich Bonhoeffer's life. The three of us read it at the same time and compared notes. The minute each brother finished, he wrote me a thank you note, telling me what he loved about the book and why it meant so much to him. I put their notes in my copy of the book and will keep them forever.

There is something about hearing the words *thank you* that can make all the difference in how we feel, how we act, how we look at life. There's no way to prove this, but I wouldn't be surprised if I have every thank you note that was ever written to me. They are scattered throughout my journal pages, and I often read them again, years later. I also love hearing the words *thank you* in any language.

Just thanking someone for his or her support says volumes. It starts in childhood. Remember that little rhyme? "If I can count on you, and you can count on me, just think what a wonderful world this will be."

Someday, when my life is over, I'd like to be remembered for three things, that I was gracious, generous, and grateful. If I can achieve that, I'll feel like I've lived a life of meaning and richness. Golda Meir once said, "Create the kind of self that you will be happy to live with all your life." That's what I've tried to do. We can have money, fame, comfort, belongings, titles, and all that comes with each of those, but if we are not grateful or generous, we've missed the mark of being happy. And if we don't treat other people graciously, we'll never have friends. Max Lucado puts it beautifully: "The people who make a difference are not the ones with the credentials, but the ones with the concern." Preach it, Max! Let's not ever forget, authentic happiness is independent of external conditions. It's based on who we are inside.

My favorite holiday every year is Thanksgiving. That's been the case as far back as I can remember because Thanksgiving requires nothing but grateful hearts. All we do to celebrate this wonderful day is think of the things for which we are grateful—all the things that make us happy to be alive. Oh, we *can* decorate and fix a big meal for friends or relatives—or go to *their* house for dinner—but the commemoration is in the attitude of gratitude, a spirit of happiness not based on external conditions.

My prayer is that everyone reading this chapter (and this book, for that matter) will experience a rich life, filled with thanksgiving and love. The best way to describe my hope for you has already been written in Romans 12:3, so I close my last simple secret with that:

> I'm speaking to you out of deep gratitude for all that God has given me, and especially as I have responsibilities in relation to you. Living then, as every one of you does, in pure grace, it's important that you not misinterpret yourselves as people who are bringing this goodness to God. No, God brings it all to you. The only accurate way to understand ourselves is by what God is and by what he does for us, not by what we are and what we do for him.

May the Lord give you a long and happy life filled to the brim with grace and gratitude.

About the Author

No one enjoys herself more than Luci Swindoll. She's full of anticipation, fun, and a sense of adventure that just won't quit. Her exuberant love for life has seen her through a career as a corporate executive at Mobil Oil (long before it became ExxonMobil), fifteen years as a chorister with the Dallas Opera, and a stint as vice president of public relations at her brother Chuck Swindoll's ministry, Insight for Living.

One of Women of Faith's original speakers, Luci has been inspiring women in conference audiences across North America for sixteen years. She has traveled to fifty-three countries on every continent and (in her words), "speaks just enough Italian and German to chat with friends and order lunch." She is the author of more than a dozen books and curriculum studies.

Luci lives in Texas in a home she designed that's part art gallery, part library, part studio, and all Luci.

Other Books by Luci Swindoll

Doing Life Differently

Free Inside and Out (with Marilyn Meberg)

The Best Devotions of Luci Swindoll

Life! Celebrate It: Listen, Learn, Laugh, Love

Notes to a Working Woman:
Finding Balance, Passion, and Fulfillment in Your Life

I Married Adventure

I Married Adventure Journal

You Bring the Confetti, God Brings the Joy

Celebrating Life: Catching the Thieves Who Steal Your Joy

After You're Dressed for Success:
A Guide to Developing Character as Well as a Career

The Alchemy of the Heart:
Life's Refining Process to Free Us from Ourselves

Wide My World, Narrow My Bed

Also available from
LUCI SWINDOLL

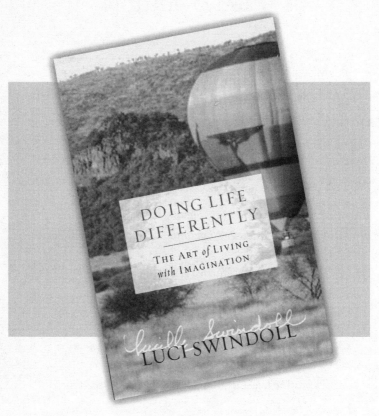

DOING LIFE
DIFFERENTLY

The Art of Living
with Imagination

LUCI SWINDOLL

"*Adventure is an attitude, not a behavior.*"

Available in your local bookstore
and in ebook format.